MAGAZINES

INSIDE & OUT

Steven Heller & Teresa Fernandes

Library of Applied Design   An Imprint of PBC INTERNATIONAL, INC.

Distributor to the book trade in the United States and Canada

Rizzoli International Publications Inc.

through St. Martin's Press

175 Fifth Avenue

New York, NY 10010

Distributor to the art trade in the United States and Canada

PBC International, Inc.

One School Street

Glen Cove, NY 11542

Distributor throughout the rest of the world

Hearst Books International

1350 Avenue of the Americas

New York, NY 10019

Library of Congress Cataloging-in-Publication Data

Magazines: inside & out / Steven Heller & Teresa Fernandes.

 p. cm.

 Contents: Includes index.

 ISBN 0-86636-380-7 (alk. paper)

 1. Magazine Design-- History--20th century. I. Fernandes, Teresa.

II. Title.

Z253.5.H43 1996   95-36552

741.6'52--dc20   CIP

CAVEAT-Information in this text is believed accurate, and will pose
no problem for the student or casual reader. However, the author
was often constrained by information contained in signed release
forms, information that could have been in error or not included at
all. Any misinformation (or lack of information) is the result of failure in these attestations. The author has done whatever is possible
to insure accuracy.

Color separation by Fine Arts Repro House Co., Ltd., Hong Kong

Printing and binding by Dai Nippan Co. (H.K.) Ltd. Hong Kong

Design by Teresa Fernandes

Art Production by Daniel Drennan

Photography for cover and chapter openers by Geoff Spear

Photography of magazines by Tom Mylroie

Research by Christine Thompson, Karen Mynatt, Jessica Hartshorn

Printed in Hong Kong

10 9 8 7 6 5 4 3 2 1

To Bradbury Thompson

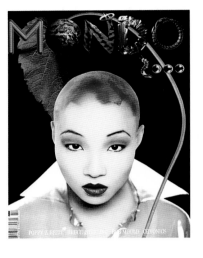

TABLE OF

CONTENTS

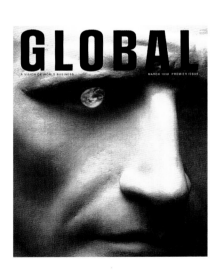

DESIGN
AND GUILT
INSIDE
AND OUT

MAGAZINE GUILT IS caused by an increasing abundance of barely read or ignored periodicals which over a short time begin to form into large piles like mold on week-old bread. The only cure for this malady is removing the menacing heaps to the recycling bin. However, this prescription is easier said than done. Magazines are habit forming, and while the excruciating pressure to read them mounts as the piles grow, most subscribers can't bear to own up to the fact that time will rarely allow for more than a casual glance. The notion that someone cannot even make time to read a magazine contributes to personal anxiety. One might justify not reading books because they require considerable concentration and long-term commitment, but magazines are collections of relatively short takes that theoretically can be consumed and digested in a fraction of the time. The impossibility of reading something so comparatively trifling as a magazine rocks even the most emotionally stable person.

Yet contributing to this problem is the fact that in the 1990s more magazines are being published than ever in the history of publishing. Considering that paper is increasingly

more expensive, electronic and digital media are fiercely competing for audiences and advertisers, and pundits have long professed the inevitable death of print, there is an amazingly large number of periodicals currently available for what appears to be a diminishing consumer base. Nevertheless, the old chestnut that this remains an essentially print culture is true. Yet this is not, however, a generalized culture, but rather one that addresses very specialized wants. Although television long ago obviated the need for mammoth general weekly magazines, like *Life*, *Look*, and *The Saturday Evening Post*, readers have fine-tuned their individual interests, and responding magazines now devote themselves exclusively to specific themes — everything from advertising to zoology. If an individual reader is curious about a variety of subjects, then an average of between five to ten specialized magazines enter the home either by subscription, newsstand purchase, or complimentary distribution. Of these, probably half are skimmed, and less are read. And with such intense competition among magazines for attention not just on the newsstand but in the home, a tremendous weight is placed on the magazine's design to entice, engage, and grab the reader.

Design has always been an important editorial component, but beginning in the 1960s, when the magazine industry was initially threatened by television, it has taken on the proportions of a miracle cure — at the same time it can also be a deadly disease. Design is what differentiates one magazine from another, although in some cases a unique design is appropriated by competitors to signal that they too belong to a particular genre. For example, in the late 1960s the then unique design of *New York* magazine was both celebrated and imitated around the nation. *New York* magazine was an original concept in regional magazine publishing — the first city service- and news-oriented weekly to offer honest consumer reports and serious journalism to its readers. The original design was an amalgam of different formats that nevertheless resulted in a truly distinctive look. It was this look — its three-column grid, standardized Egyptian headlines topped by heavy scotch rules, and a generous number of Times Roman pull quotes, as well as consistently sophisticated conceptual illustration and photography — that became the code that other city magazines adopted; not unlike the way local radio and television stations adopt the same basic on-air formats. While *New York* magazine's editorial thrust was strong enough to set it apart from the rest of the field, its overall design was the deciding and most iconic factor in forging its distinctive personality. There are a handful of other magazines throughout the '60s and '70s worth noting for their unique (indeed memorable) design formats: *Harper's Bazaar*, brilliantly and distinctively designed in the 1950s by maestro Alexey Brodovitch, gave way to exceptional typographic and conceptual approaches by, in order of succession, Henry Wolf, Marvin Israel, and the duo of Bea Fietler and Ruth Ansel. *Esquire*, art directed in the late 1950s by Henry Wolf, the early 1960s by Sam Antupit, and in the mid-1970s by Robert Priest each established standards of magazine design excellence. Priest's striking "post-Modern" typographic mannerism for *Esquire* also fostered countless other magazine design imitations.

Without design a magazine is merely a melange of disparate elements; with it, it is a disciplined entity. Therefore all magazines are designed in some way or another — for better or worse — and design should be critically discussed as either being bad or good. The latter is characterized by an overall intelligent scheme, including lively pacing (the manner in which the editorial material flows seamlessly from one story to the next), authoritative typography, sophisticated visuals, and an element of surprise. The former is noted for jarring pacing, inelegant typography, toss-away

visuals, and an overall lack of attention to detail. Curiously, not all important magazines are well designed. For decades *Time* magazine was designed in a default manner by layout editors, not designers per se, who rigidly followed an already tight layout plan. In the 1960s, while *Time* attempted to visually conform to the times, it had not made even the slightest fundamental changes that would signal a new design intelligence. But by the mid-1970s, finally, *Time* was completely recast by a strong design director (Walter Bernard) so that it retained its news quality but became more reader accessible through design elements and ideas. The original *Life* magazine also premiered in the 1930s with a rather neutral design format which competently framed its powerful photography, but as time wore on the format not only frayed at the edges but lost any design distinction. When *Life* was revived after having folded for a brief period in the 1970s more emphasis was placed on its typography and layout as a significant editorial enhancement, and today it is an exemplary mix of design and image.

By the 1980s design was inextricably wed to the editorial personalities of most magazines. It had become so important that many magazines no longer hired mere art directors to devise their formats, but rather engaged a new breed of professional, the design consultant. Prior to this evolutionary stage an art director worked on one magazine for a relatively long time, and with a staff of designers, made whatever changes — major and minor — that were demanded. Conversely, the design consultant is an outsider hired for his or her expertise, who builds a design scheme based on the editorial (and advertising) requirements of the magazine as expressed by its publisher, editor, and art director. Sometimes this is a tight fit with all parties in perfect accord, other times the design preferences and prejudices of the consultant are affixed to the problem without necessarily being a workable solution. But whatever the outcome, the fact that consultants are used at all indicates a respect, if not awe, of the power of design.

The dark side of this phenomenon is that along with respect, much weight is placed on design. Some believe design alone propels a magazine's success, ignoring other editorial factors. When design works it does so in harmony with editorial content. But when a magazine is faltering, often the design is the most overt manifestation and therefore projected as the cause of failure. Herein, of course, lies a major misconception. A magazine is only as good as its content, and while design may enhance content, it rarely replaces it. Even a visual magazine is beholden to its visual content, not the design frame in which it is presented. When design is blamed for the ills caused by editorial incompetence it is scrapped in favor of another design which often reveals a kind of schizophrenia (and the substitute design may not do the job, either). Like those who suffer from multiple personalities, a magazine that shifts design schemes too often loses the identity it needs to succeed. On the other hand, this should not imply that a magazine's design is always a perfect fit. The venerable *Rolling Stone* has had at least half a dozen design reincarnations, some more viable than others. Prior to the current, unmistakable though continually eclectic scheme developed by design director Fred Woodward, *Rolling Stone* was somewhat adrift. Its design, like other magazines of the early 1980s, was couched in a retro sensibility that provided a look, but not a personality. *Rolling Stone* appeared to be generic rather than exude the distinctive presence it does today as America's premier music culture magazine. In this sense a new scheme to reinstate its design personality was necessary. Although Woodward's design shifts in terms of style, the overall scheme, based on classic typefaces used in an early iteration of the magazine, gives it a needed anchor.

But some magazines are redesigned for no other reason than a new editor or publisher wants to make his or her mark — and design is the most obvious (and easiest) means to achieve this. A magazine's design may not be broken, but regardless it will be fixed. In such cases graphic design becomes little more than a replacement part, a cog in the wheel of survival. While design need not be immutable, it should provide the stasis that readers require to find their ways. If a magazine is true to its root word, *magazin*, and is a metaphor for a storehouse with showrooms filled with aisles of goods, then a design is not only the decoration for the store, but the navigational device that provides "customers" with familiar signposts in the midst of various surprises. Indeed magazines of the 1960s and '70s were true to the notion that an overall design should last for some time, while individual features might change and shift from issue to issue.

In the '90s, however, this is no longer the golden rule of magazine design. While most regularly issued magazines (weeklies and monthlies) maintain invariant envelopes in which an array of editorial contents are placed, many "alternative" publications are experimenting with totally mutable design schemes, and sometimes overall sizes and shapes. For some, consistency has become the hobgoblin of creativity, and so a new breed of magazine, usually cultural or artistic in scope, has developed that eschews any semblance of rigidity. Perhaps the only concession to tradition is a consistent logo; but even logos — the most identifiable component of magazine design — are known to change to echo or contrast with a cover artwork or design. Although the majority of these mutable magazines are geared to a youthful audience, those like *Ray Gun* have had an influence on the mainstream as well.

Although it's improbable that *Ray Gun*'s typographic anarchy will make its way to *Esquire*, *The New York Times Magazine*, or other well-designed, but decidedly "establishment" journals, it has nevertheless inspired broader typographic leeway in a wide range of magazines. It has also spawned many imitators — the excellent students do their master proud, while others blindly mimic the surface characteristics without the original's soul. Similarly, *Emigre* has been a wellspring of experimental graphics with an influence that far exceeds its meager pressrun and readership. Through its introduction and distribution of exclusive typefaces, the *Emigre* aesthetic has been adopted by many magazines that seek either hip codes or more honestly want to push proscribed limits on their own. New approaches to magazine design come and go, some become history, some are forgotten, but some are adopted and become new additions to the old standards.

Unlike the postwar years of magazine design — which some refer to as the "Golden Years" because this was the time when modernism and eclecticism combined to make the printed page a melange of elegance and playfulness — there are many more options for publication design today than at any time in history. The traditional canon has long ago been replaced by unconventional conventions. The magazines selected for MAGAZINES: INSIDE AND OUT represent the diversity not just of subject, but of visual approach. Sure, there are probably an equal number of magazines in the world — indeed in countries not even represented in this sampling — that produce exceptionally designed magazines. But the reason for making these selections is not to show all the award winners, but how various methods are practiced; how certain current styles are reinterpreted by different designers; how unique design identities are established; and how conceptual thinking pervades the design of the best magazines. The periodicals here should not be compared against one another; although there are a number in the same subject category (and a few even doing the same jobs for the same audiences), each

must be viewed on its own merits, for how the material is presented in terms of typography, page layout, pacing, and illustration. Even though *Rolling Stone* and *Ray Gun* are music culture magazines, they address their themes and audiences with distinctive voices — one does not negate the other. Even though *Eye*, *Graphis*, and *Gráphica* are all graphic design magazines, they have carved out distinctive identities which allow them to approach the material differently, each with valid points of view. As this book is used it should be read as an overview of relatively successful magazines. Not with reference to circulation or advertising (although that is not to be totally ignored), but in terms of how these use the power of design to communicate their messages.

However, not even magnificent design can cure magazine guilt. When *Colors*, *Rolling Stone*, *Garbage*, *Life*, and *Martha Stewart*'s *Living* come into the home all in the same week, there is no way that the average person will be able to skim, no less read them all — and by the time the next batch arrives the preceding may hardly be touched. But good design will make the difference in how a magazine is ultimately perceived. If a magazine is compelling enough, the reader may be forced to make the time. The design of the magazines included in MAGAZINES: INSIDE AND OUT each demands attention.

For those who are or will be publication designers these examples provide models for how the traditional and experimental, the classical and the new wave approaches can be used to maximum, and maybe guiltless, effect.

—Steven Heller

ABITARE
AdD:
ANY
A|R|C
ARCHIS
ART ISSUES.
AZURE
BLIND SPOT
BLUEPRINT
C MAGAZINE
CANADIAN ART
EMIGRE

ART, ARCHITECTURE & DESIGN

EYE
GARDEN DESIGN
GRÁFICA
GRAPHIS
GUGGENHEIM MAGAZINE
INTERIOR DESIGN OUTLOOK
METALSMITH
METROPOLIS
NOZONE
O-ZONE
PICTOPIA
RUBBER BLANKET
U&lc
WORLD ART

"and we like it the way it is"

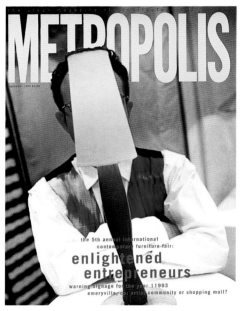

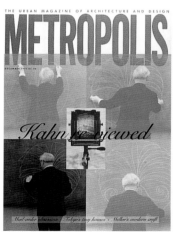

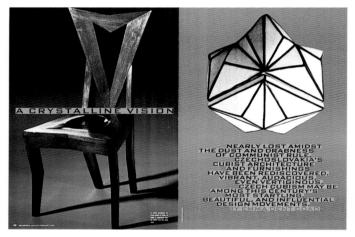

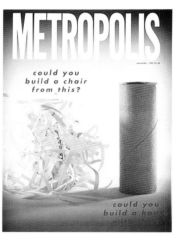

PUBLISHER
BELLEROPHON
PUBLICATION
ART DIRECTORS
NANCY KRUGER COHEN
CARL LEHMANN-HAUPT
PHOTOGRAPHERS
KRISTINE LARSEN
MARTIN E. RICH, AIA
BILL STEELE
VITRA MUSEUM
THE WILDERSTEIN
PRESERVATION SOCIETY
DAN WINTERS

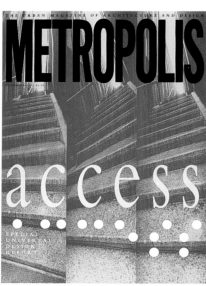

12

USA
METROPOLIS

MANY CULTURE MAGAZINES lay claim to the distinction of having introduced post-modern or new-wave graphics to publication design, but even if *Metropolis* was not the very first, it is certainly one of the most significant. It is now one of the last so-called culture tabs, the tabloid-sized, web-printed, largely color magazine born in the late '70s and early '80s. A magazine for professional and lay people who are concerned with design and design issues, *Metropolis* focuses on interior, landscape, graphic, furniture, and architectural design and visually interprets these distinct cultural manifestations through cutting-edge typographics, inventive picture juxtapositions, and computer-imaging techniques. Although the magazine's basic architecture remains constant in the front and back of the book, the feature well changes radically every issue, sometimes to distinguish one disparate article from the next, other times to give identity to a collection of thematic stories. In addition, *Metropolis*'s cover designs are always pushing convention, from a staid but elegant photograph one issue, to a rave typographic number the next. Here is a magazine caught in the vortex of style that has managed to overcome its constraints with continually growing, responsive graphic design.

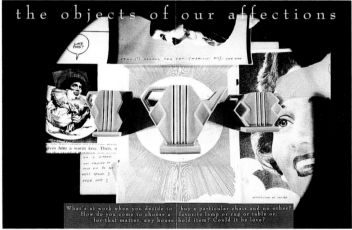

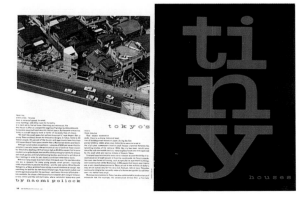

PUBLISHER
BELLEROPHON PUBLICATION
ART DIRECTORS
NANCY KRUGER COHEN
CARL LEHMANN-HAUPT
PHOTOGRAPHERS
CHIP KIDD
YUTAKA SUZUKI
DAN WINTERS
ILLUSTRATORS
TERRY GILLIAM
CHIP KIDD

O-ZONE

DEVOTED TO FANTASTIC ART and editorial illustration, this exquisite magazine takes the world's finest applied art out of its often subsidiary role to text and gives it center stage. And what a stage set it is: the cover is a mini-poster with a handsome, contemporary logo that combines classic Bodoni with a bold Futura. The *o* in zone is a bull's-eye that draws the viewer's eye into the image. A detail of an illustration screams off the page announcing a featured artist, and serving as a testament to the artistic integrity of powerful illustration. Inside spreads fulfill Alexey Brodovitch's now famous command about magazine art direction, "Astonish me!" In the manner of Brodovitch, renowned as art director of *Harper's Bazaar* in the 1950s and '60s, *O-Zone*'s typography is classic Bodoni set against the boldest pictorial elements. Since this is a magazine of images, the type must serve a neutral function. But rather than invisible, the Bodoni is used as an expressive device to complement, frame, and otherwise enhance the images displayed. *O-Zone* serves many roles, as showcase, portfolio, experiment, but also as proof that when used with a contemporary spirit, classic typography is without equal.

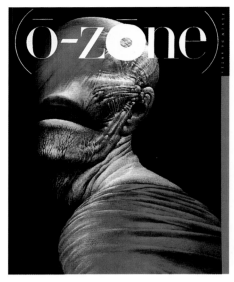

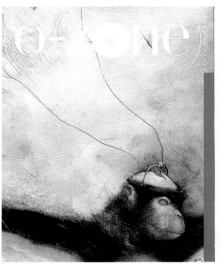

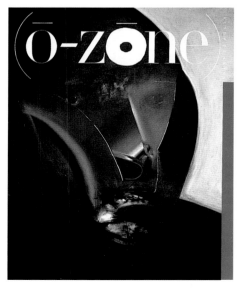

PUBLISHER
CASA DE IDEIAS
CREATIVE DIRECTOR
**OSWALDO MIRANDA
(MIRAN)**
ART DIRECTOR
**OSWALDO MIRANDA
(MIRAN)**
DESIGNER
**OSWALDO MIRANDA
(MIRAN)**
ILLUSTRATORS
**MARSHALL ARISMAN
BRAD HOLLAND
MATT MAHURIN
WIESLAW WALKUSKI**

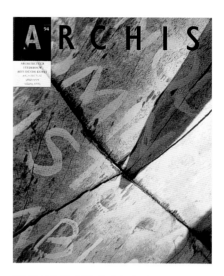

ARCHIS

"FROM THE APPEARANCE of the first issue in 1986 until the last issue of 1992 the graphic and typographical design of *Archis* has remained the same...," states *Archis*'s editor about a change in format. "The design was based on a clear presentation of text and artwork, brought together in a layout in which the accent was on the treatment of the text as content." This Dutch-based bilingual journal of architecture was built on an immutable grid both because design was viewed as a servant to the text and image, and because publishing in two languages is unwieldy at best. The Dutch text set in Plantijn and the English in Gill Sans gave the pages functional and aesthetic contrast. About its economical presentation *Archis*'s editor states: "As tempting as it is to posture amongst the brightly-colored splays of the international magazines, it is just as dangerous to present the incongruous figure of a parrot in a body stocking." In this sense *Archis* balances the need to look contemporary with the desire to appear unphased by fashion and design technology.

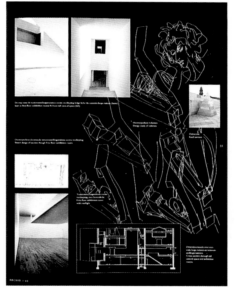

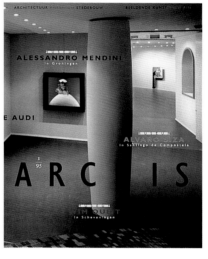

PUBLISHER
**NETHERLANDS ARCHI-
TECTURE INSTITUTE &
MISSET PUBLISHERS**
ART DIRECTOR
HERMAN DE VRIES
DESIGNER
HERMAN DE VRIES
ARTISTS
**ALIGHIERO E BOETTI
ALESSANDRO MENDINI
WIM QUIST/ARCHITEK-
TENBURO QUIST
MARCOS LORA READ
ALVARO SIZA**
PHOTOGRAPHERS
**MAURICE BRANDTS
MARC DUBOIS
PAUL VAN LOENEN
PAOLO MUSSAT SARTOR
SIEBE SWART**

RUBBER BLANKET

IN RECENT YEARS the comic book has been transformed into the graphic novel and the comics magazine has found new forms. *Rubber Blanket* is case in point. It was created as a workshop in which to explore the potential of comics as a story-telling medium, and in so doing attract new readers who did not normally read comics. "The main challenge was to design a comics magazine that didn't look like a comic book — with all its negative connotations," says its editor and publisher. Yet even for the comics aficionado the content was unusual for the field, so the design had to reflect this anomaly and still say "comics." From its eye-catching cover image and custom logo (that changes every issue) to the limited variety of comic styles inside, *Rubber Blanket* exudes its own identity within an over-crowded genre. But to describe it solely in design terms is difficult. Basic architecture and typography are overshadowed by the style and content of the material. Indeed high production values — fine printing and good paper — are key to this distinction; its two-color interior printing (sometimes to give a chiaroscuro effect) separates *Rubber Blanket* from full-color comic books and black and white alternative comics. The magazine's sardonic motto: "If we don't treat comics as garbage, maybe you won't" is strictly adhered to.

PUBLISHER
RUBBER BLANKET PRESS
ART DIRECTORS
RICHMOND LEWIS
DAVID MAZZUCCHELLI
DESIGNERS
RICHMOND LEWIS
DAVID MAZZUCCHELLI
ILLUSTRATOR
DAVID MAZZUCCHELLI

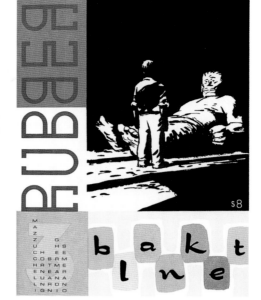

PUBLISHER
**RUBBER BLANKET
PRESS**
ART DIRECTORS
**RICHMOND LEWIS
DAVID MAZZUCCHELLI**
DESIGNERS
**RICHMOND LEWIS
DAVID MAZZUCCHELLI
TED STEARN**
ILLUSTRATORS
**RICHMOND LEWIS
DAVID MAZZUCCHELLI
TED STEARN**

envirobeat

AZURE

IT IS INTERESTING to chart the evolution of an architecture and design magazine. How does it conform to or interpret the current issues? Does it follow or set standards? In *Azure*'s case the covers are indicators of this evolutionary process. Those from 1993 and 1994 suggest a certain comfort in the neoclassical trends in design. Its typographic scheme is based on Bodoni (although its logo is a squat and elongated gothic). By 1995, however, the type is almost all slammed gothics (including a redesigned logo that owes a certain flair to *Life* magazine). The color scheme has also changed to the dirty pastels that have become popular of late. *Azure* is the quintessential magazine of its time. Not an innovator, in any way, it certainly follows the road well traveled with a great deal of panache. Its interior design, replete with overlapping, variously colored headlines, is set against a perfectly readable four-column grid of flush left/rag right Bodoni. Small images pervade, rather than large central images which are reserved for the cover.

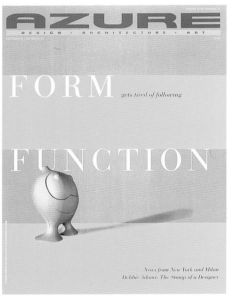
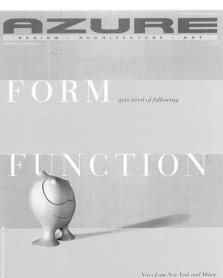

FORM *gets tired of following*

FUNCTION

News from New York and Milan
Debbie Adams: The Stamp of a Designer

PUBLISHER
AZURE PUBLISHING INC.
ART DIRECTORS
DITI KATONA
JOHN PYLPCZAK
DESIGNERS
SUSAN McINTEE
JOHN PYLPCZAK
PHOTOGRAPHERS
JOËL BÉNARD
ROB DAVIDSON
DAVID WHITTAKER

Report from Germany

Orgatec

Thema Domus

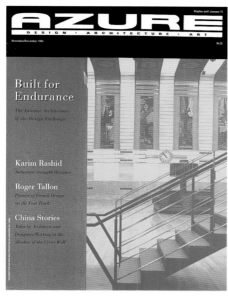

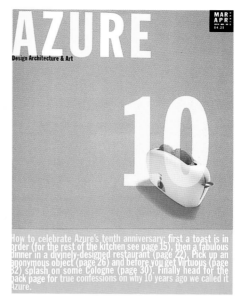

PUBLISHER
AZURE PUBLISHING INC.
ART DIRECTORS
DITI KATONA
JOHN PYLPCZAK
DESIGNERS
SUSAN McINTEE
JOHN PYLPCZAK
PHOTOGRAPHERS
STEVEN EVANS
ROMAN PYLYPCZAK
ILLUSTRATOR
JEFF JACKSON

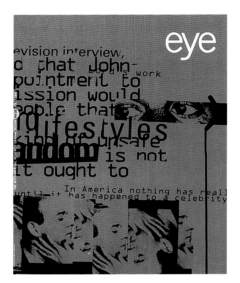

EYE

A GRAPHIC DESIGN magazine can be a graphically designed "experience," like *Emigre*, or a comparatively neutral vessel; *Eye* is the latter. But that does not mean it is without identity. Adopting a more conventional format — a clearly defined front and back of the book and feature well with three-column grid, consistent headline, subhead, body, and caption typefaces — provides a forum for rather diverse subject matter. The magazine frames the featured design sometimes as distinct portfolios others as illustrations of the articles. Visuals are important — from the iconographic cover (often a detail of an inside work) to the documentary examples inside — but text is paramount. Although *Eye* reports on contemporary, cutting-edge design it does not mimic any of those characteristics, such as layering, smashing, and digital distortion. *Eye*'s typography is straightforwardly functional, with shifts in scale and the occasional subtle typographic tweak of a letter or word for increased emphasis. With symphonic skill feature articles are purposefully paced so that visual impact reaches its height by the middle of the well and slowly winds down to a coda by the end — often as a text-heavy essay. Nevertheless, consistency is not a hobgoblin, but the hero of *Eye*'s unique personality.

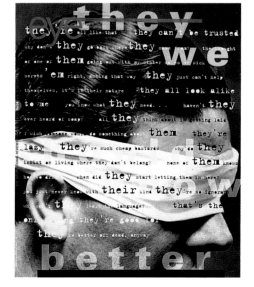

PUBLISHERS
**EMAP BUSINESS
COMMUNICATIONS LTD.
WORDSEARCH LTD.**
ART DIRECTOR
STEPHEN COATES
DESIGNER
STEPHEN COATES

A sense of
rupture

PUBLISHERS
**EMAP BUSINESS
COMMUNICATIONS LTD.
WORDSEARCH LTD.**
ART DIRECTOR
STEPHEN COATES
DESIGNER
STEPHEN COATES

Form and purpose

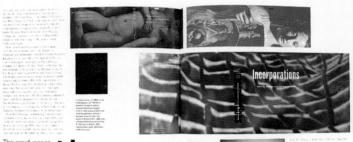

Incorporations

The producer as
author

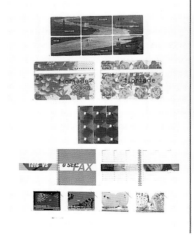

CANADIAN ART

TAKING A CONSERVATIVE course with an art magazine can be safe or treacherous. Safe because it does not interfere (or interpret) the art under scrutiny; treacherous because it can give a possibly wrong, stodgy impression. In this case, the low-key approach is handled gingerly with occasional tips of the hat to the new wave when the subject demands it. The format, which is reminiscent of a news magazine's feature well, does not rely on tricks, but uses shifts in typographic styles to suggest the subjects being covered. Full-color photographs of artists in their workspaces and exhibitions further add a journalistic sensibility to the magazine. Artworks are also straightforwardly shown so as not to intrude on the aesthetic integrity of the piece. Framed by generous white space, *Canadian Art* magazine is a paragon of appropriateness.

PUBLISHER
THE CANADIAN ART FOUNDATION/KEY PUBLISHERS CO., LTD.
ART DIRECTOR
JOHN ORMSBY
DESIGNER
JOHN ORMSBY
PHOTOGRAPHERS
JOHN VERE BROWN
NIGEL DICKSON

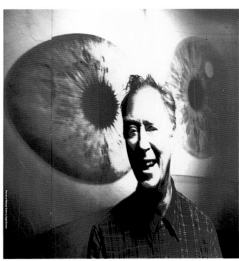

Dorothea
Rockburne's

by Murray Pomerance

[Quantum]

A northern star rises in the southern firmament

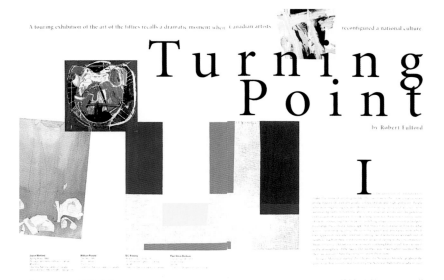

John Massey's
artistic career may be one of the most uncomfortable on record

No Exit

John Bentley Mays investigates

A touring exhibition of the art of the fifties recalls a dramatic moment when Canadian artists   reconfigured a national culture

Turning
Point
I

by Robert Fulford

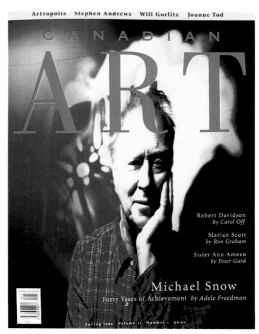

Artropolis • Stephen Andrews • Will Gorlitz • Joanne Tod

CANADIAN ART

Robert Davidson
by Carol Off

Marian Scott
by Ron Graham

Sister Ann Ameen
by Peter Gard

Michael Snow
Forty Years of Achievement *by Adele Freedman*

Spring 1994   Volume 11   Number 1 $6.00

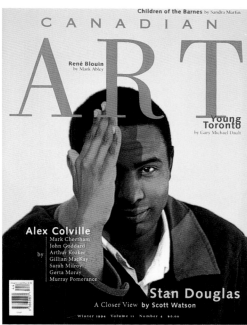

Children of the Barnes by Sandra Martin

CANADIAN ART

René Blouin
by Mark Abley

**Young
Toronto**
by Gary Michael Dault

Alex Colville
by
Mark Cheetham
John Goddard
Arthur Kroker
Gillian MacKay
Sarah Milroy
Gerta Moray
Murray Pomerance

Stan Douglas
A Closer View *by Scott Watson*

Winter 1994   Volume 11   Number 4 $6.00

PUBLISHER
**THE CANADIAN ART
FOUNDATION/KEY PUB-
LISHERS CO., LTD.**
ART DIRECTOR
JOHN ORMSBY
DESIGNER
JOHN ORMSBY
PHOTOGRAPHERS
**JAN PETER BÖNNING
NIGEL DICKSON
EDEN ROBBINS
BRIAN SMALE**

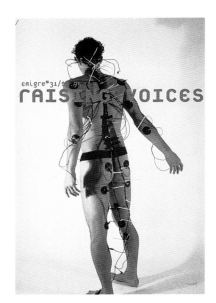

USA

EMIGRE

THIS PIONEER of digital type design
has earned its place as both the clarion
of the New Typography and a leading experimental design showcase. While it
was begun as an alternative culture journal, *Emigre* soon found a niche as the
laboratory of contemporary graphic
design in which its own typefaces and
those of other desktop type founders
were used in context, not simply as conventional line samples. Emigre does not
maintain a consistent format, although it
does have an unmistakable personality.
Whether designed by editor Rudy VanderLans or by frequent guest designers,
Emigre avoids magazine conventions.
In its original tabloid form (in 1995 it
changed to a smaller, standard magazine
size) columns composed with varying
types would splash across an entire
page, or if set in columns might smash
against each other in a rejection of gut-
ters or column rules. Although the logo
is relatively constant, the predominantly
two- and three-color covers printed on a
toothy matte stock radically change each
issue to reflect the inside content or a
featured designer. Rather than a magazine, *Emigre* might best be described as
an ever-changing gallery of ideas.

PUBLISHER
EMIGRE
ART DIRECTOR
RUDY VANDERLANS
DESIGNERS
RUDY VANDERLANS
PHOTOGRAPHERS
RUDY VANDERLANS
ALISON WHITE

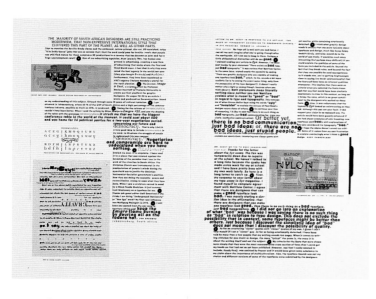

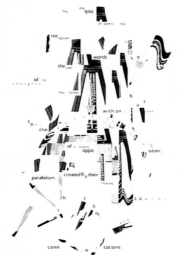

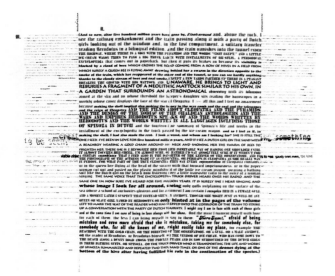

PUBLISHER
EMIGRE
ART DIRECTOR
RUDY VANDERLANS
EDITOR
JEFFERY KEEDY
DESIGNERS
THE DESIGNERS
REPUBLIC
TONY KLASSEN
CONOR MANGAT
JAMES STOECKER
GAIL SWANLUND
RICK VALECENTI
RUDY VANDERLANS
ILLUSTRATORS
DAVID ISRAEL
MICHAEL KIPPENHAN

PUBLISHER
NOZONE
ART DIRECTOR
KNICKERBOCKER
DESIGNER
KNICKERBOCKER
ILLUSTRATORS
RON BARRETT
GARY BASEMAN
FLY
DAVID GOLDIN
JONATHON ROSEN
JOOST SWARTE

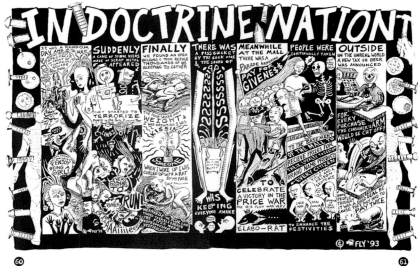

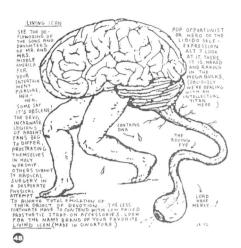

USA

NOZONE

THE DESIGNER ASSERTS that *Nozone*'s "aesthetic goal is to combine grit with elegance, achieved by designing with Xeroxes and X-Actos while printing on expensive papers." In fact, this irregularly published collection of visual essays and comic strips is what it promises, a kind of sweet and sour or yin and yang of publishing. The overall design decisions are made in relation to its size, shape, and color. One issue is a tabloid; another a small square with a die-cut cover; a third a perfect-bound paperback book. The principle design elements are the artworks and comics themselves, each varied style — drawing, lettering, typography — is sewn into the whole in a kind of graphic arts patch-quilt. *Nozone* derives from a genre of underground comics and alternative magazines, but it is not totally beholden to that tradition. Through the material selected and the pacing of the individual components, *Nozone* assumes its own identity. It contains no advertising to muck up its deliberate chaos. And although its logo constantly changes — indeed in its paperback issue it is subtly displayed — this magazine is very recognizable in its popular genre.

PUBLISHER
NOZONE
ART DIRECTOR
KNICKERBOCKER
DESIGNER
KNICKERBOCKER
ILLUSTRATORS
GARY BASEMAN
MARK MAREK
JONATHON ROSEN

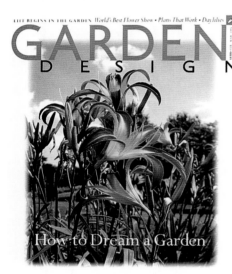

PUBLISHER
**MEIGHER
COMMUNICATIONS**
CREATIVE DIRECTOR
MICHAEL GROSSMAN
ART DIRECTOR
PAUL ROELOFS
PHOTOGRAPHERS
**CHRISTOPHER BAKER
ALAN L. DETRICK
DEBORAH JONES
KEN ROBBINS**

GARDEN DESIGN

MANY MAGAZINES ARE relaunched and redesigned with an eye towards attracting younger audiences. In this sense *Garden Design* could easily have been recast with trendy design tropes, but was not. Instead, it was given a unique format which is contemporary without being slavishly faddish. The idea was to present exemplary residential landscapes in a way that would interest the generalist. This was accomplished editorially by creating lively front of the book departments, "Dirt" (news and commentary), "Growing" (facts and figures), "Design" (profiles and factoids), and "Leaves" (classics of garden literature). Each section is distinctively formatted with various borders, illustrations, and icons, yet typographically consistent with the whole. Color is generously used throughout for both images and text. The feature articles are tied together by the typefaces, but spreads change according to subject. Original landscape photography is the major visual component, including gorgeous panoramas as well as minute garden details. What distinguishes *Garden Design* from other garden magazines is its harmony between graphics and photographs, and fealty to the idea that this magazine is not simply about pretty surroundings but rather landscape design.

HERBARY by Susanna Moore

Miracle Worker

A LEGENDARY HEALER, ALOE VERA COOLS, SOOTHES, AND SALVES

A stiff-leafed, tall, spiky aloe vera was given to me once by a Peruvian friend when I badly burned my leg. My doctor had prescribed a tetanus shot and antibiotics, and she told me that a skin graft would be necessary. I took the medicine. I also cut a slender leaf from the aloe and kept it in a jar of water. Each day, I would cut an inch from the bottom of the plant, the knife moving easily through the flesh of the leaf. I would carefully peel away the outer green skin and collect the viscous, clear-colored gel. Quickly, before it could slide through my fingers, I would hold it to the wound, which I then bound with gauze. As I made the poultice each day, I became my own shaman, regressing confidently to a state of calm belief.

I understood then why Alexander the Great had bothered to claim a tiny aloe-covered island off the coast of Somalia on behalf of his soldiers. I knew, as I held the cool, miraculous plant to my wound, why, in the sixth century, Arab traders had sailed as far as China to sell aloe in the bazaars—and why Native American medicine men hid the secrets of what they called the mystery plant.

Aloe has long proved to be a cooling treatment for sunburn. It causes burns to lose their sting. It soothes frostbite and rashes, as well as helps to heal minor wounds—thanks to a substance known as allantoin. As

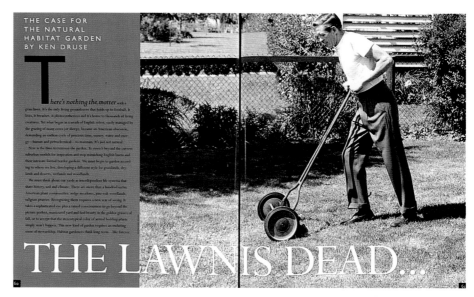

THE CASE FOR THE NATURAL HABITAT GARDEN BY KEN DRUSE

There's nothing the matter with a grass lawn. It's the only living groundcover that holds up to football. It lives, it breathes, it photosynthesizes and it's home to thousands of living creatures. Yet what began as a swath of English velvet, easily managed by the grazing of many cows (or sheep), became an American obsession, demanding an endless cycle of precious time, money, water and energy—human and petrochemical—to maintain. It's just not natural.

Now is the time to reinvent the garden. To stretch beyond the current suburban models for inspiration and stop mimicking English lawns and their intricate formal border gardens. We must begin to garden according to where we live, developing a different style for grasslands, drylands and deserts, wetlands and woodlands.

We must think about our yards as interdependent life systems that share history, soil and climate. There are more than a hundred native American plant communities: sedge meadows, pine-oak woodlands, tallgrass prairies. Recognizing them requires a new way of seeing. It takes a sophisticated eye plus a raised consciousness to go beyond the picture-perfect, manicured yard and find beauty in the golden grasses of fall, or to accept that the stereotypical color of aerial bedding plant simply won't happen. This new kind of garden requires an enduring sense of stewardship. Habitat gardeners think long term—like forever.

THE LAWN IS DEAD...

FACED WITH THE CHALLENGE OF RENOVATING A CLASSIC, CHARLES PLATT'S FAMILY MADE HIS GARDEN A PLACE WHERE NEW TRADITIONS THRIVE ON THE RICH TERRAIN OF THE PAST

THE LONG VIEW

BY DOUGLAS BRENNER • PHOTOGRAPHS BY MICK HALES

The Platts' American villas in Cornish, New Hampshire—in a survival of turn-of-the-century family photographs, left, and today, above.

GALLERY

Karl Blossfeldt

When Berlin sculptor Karl Blossfeldt (1865–1932), a late-nineteenth-century artist, published two remarkable books of photographs capturing brilliantly and intimately the gardener's universe of discovery...

BLOSSFELDT MOVED PLANT LIFE INTO THE STUDIO SETTING OF NEUTRAL BACKGROUND AND CONTROLLED LIGHT WITH GREAT EFFECT...

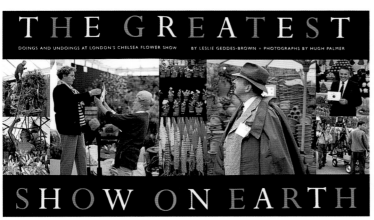

THE GREATEST

DOINGS AND UNDOINGS AT LONDON'S CHELSEA FLOWER SHOW • BY LESLIE GEDDES-BROWN • PHOTOGRAPHS BY HUGH PALMER

SHOW ON EARTH

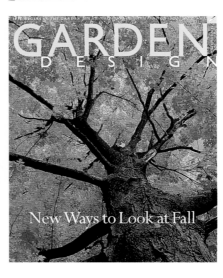

THE ORIGINS IN THE GARDEN

GARDEN DESIGN

New Ways to Look at Fall

PUBLISHER
MEIGHER COMMUNICATIONS
CREATIVE DIRECTOR
MICHAEL GROSSMAN
ART DIRECTOR
PAUL ROELOFS
PHOTOGRAPHERS
KARL BLOSSFELDT
MICK HALES
STEPHEN G. MAKA/ PHOTO/NATS
HUGH PALMER
PETRIFIED FILMS
ILLUSTRATOR
THE LIBRARY OF THE NEW YORK BOTANICAL GARDEN

PUBLISHER

**SOLOMON R. GUGGEN-
HEIM MUSEUM**

ART DIRECTOR

MASSIMO VIGNELLI

DESIGNERS

**DANI PIDERMAN
MASSIMO VIGNELLI**

ARTISTS

**ROY LICHTENSTEIN
GUSTAV KLUTSIS/
COLLECTION STATE ART
MUSEUM OF LATVIA,
KATARZYNA KOBRO/
COLLECTION MUSEUM
SZTUKI**

PHOTOGRAPHERS

**COLLECTION OF THE
MUSÉE PICASSO/ESTATE
OF J. GONZÁLES
DAVID HEALD
WILLIAM H. SHORT**

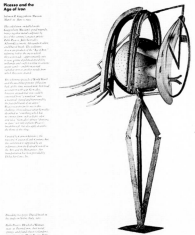

GUGGENHEIM MAGAZINE _{USA}

Zaha Hadid's Vision for The Great Utopia

In her London-based practice, Zaha Hadid has pursued the unfinished architectural revolution begun by the Russian avant-garde. Her project begins with visionary paintings in which she explores buildings and cities caught in the warp of industrial Futurism. Emerging from these speculations are always sober abstract and streamlined forms seen dynamized by invisible fields of energy. Hadid's design for the installation of The Great Utopia is a radicalization of forms and space that the Russian

PUBLISHER
**SOLOMON R. GUGGEN-
HEIM MUSEUM**
ART DIRECTOR
MASSIMO VIGNELLI
DESIGNERS
**DANI PIDERMAN
MASSIMO VIGNELLI**
PHOTOGRAPHERS
**ALDO BALLO/ ARCHIVIO
OLIVETTI CORP.
ARCHIVIO PIAGGIO V.E.
DAVID HEALD
TONI NICOLINI/ARCHIVIO
D.D.L. STUDIO/ ARCHIVIO
CASTIGLIONI
SOLOMON R. GUGGEN-
HEIM MUSEUM**

THE MOST IMPRESSIVE thing about the *Guggenheim Magazine*, New York's leading contemporary art institution's full-color, tabloid periodical for members, is that flipping through it one feels as if they are in the museum itself. This publication is so well-paced that it approximates a walk up or down the Guggenheim's famous ramped rotunda. Art, photography, and typography (a harmonious blend of classic and gothic) are inextricably wed in such a way that there is not a missed visual or editorial beat. Stories flow into one another as if the walls of a fluid gallery. White space is an elegant frame that gives way to full-bleed, mural-like pages. While totally consistent, the layouts are different insofar as each story, headlined with a Futura, has its own personality as determined by the illustrations and typographic layout. The covers radically change each issue, from the posterlike introduction, to the "Italian Metamorphosis" exhibit in which the cover type is actually painted on Fifth Avenue and photographed from above, to the monumental portrait of Frank Lloyd Wright standing on a balcony of the museum under construction. Everything about this journal is functional, handsome, and surprising.

PUBLISHER
**INTERNATIONAL TYPE-
FACE CORPORATION**
ART DIRECTOR
WOODY PIRTLE
DESIGNERS
**SARAH BLACKBURN
HAROLD BURCH
LIBBY CARTON
DONNA CHING
MATT HECK
JOHN KLOTNIA
IVETTE MONTES DE OCA**

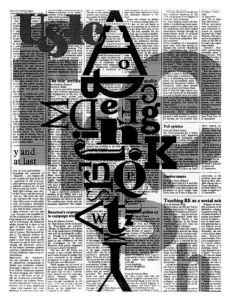

U&lc

USA

FROM AN EDITOR'S POINT of view, having a different designer totally redesign a regularly published magazine from scratch every issue is a potential nightmare. From the designer's point of view, the biggest problem would be having to work with a proscribed set of typefaces. Well, that's exactly the nature of *U&lc*. Every issue is redesigned, but each designer is limited to a range of ITC typefaces. Nevertheless that's exactly what gives this tabloid magazine devoted to typography, graphic, and digital design its unique niche. Overcoming logistical difficulties, *U&lc*'s editor has perfected the art of "expressive magazine design." Each thematic issue is a tabula rasa, and each article is uniquely designed based on the subject itself rather than any overarching design format. Here is one magazine where interiors are as surprising as covers, and the covers are totally unpredictable from issue to issue. The designers' fundamental challenge is not distinguishing issues from one another, but how to imaginatively used the ITC faces. The only design element of *U&lc* that remains constant is its logo, designed by Herb Lubalin (and only modified slightly since he founded the magazine over twenty years ago).

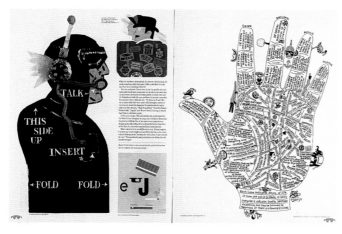

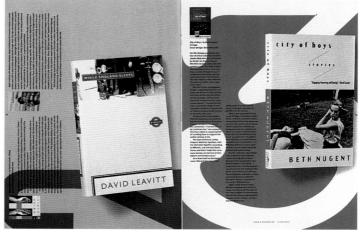

PUBLISHER
INTERNATIONAL TYPEFACE
CORPORATION
ART DIRECTORS
HAROLD BURCH, SEYMOUR
CHWAST, PAUL DAVIS
JOHN KLOTNIA
WOODY PIRTLE
DESIGNERS
CHALKEY CALDERWOOD
MYRNA DAVIS
PAUL DAVIS
CHRISTINA FREYSS
JOHN KLOTNIA
LISA MAZUR
IVETTE MONTES DE OCA
HARVETAI MUODTONS
ELAINE PETSCHEK
GREG SIMPSON
ROBERT SPICA
ILLUSTRATORS
SEYMOUR CHWAST
KING FEATURES SYNDICATE
PHOTOGRAPHY
COOPER UNION

AdD:

A MAGAZINE DEVOTED TO advertising
and graphic design is one of the most
difficult to design for since it must balance the integrity of the subject matter
with the creativity expressed in the magazine itself. *AdD:* succeeds where many
"trade" publications fail. Its graphic personality is defined by typography that
avoids self-conscious conceits and
frames the editorial material in an understated manner. Contributing to the
design problem is the use of a minimal
amount of text which ordinarily would
provide a neutral framing device. Nevertheless, this is decidedly where an
intelligent format helps telegraph the
standards by which material is selected.
Just as the magazine's design must not
compete with the material being shown,
the advertisements and designs selected
for inclusion cannot fall below the level
of competence and excellence displayed
in the magazine as a whole.

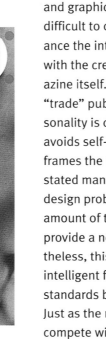

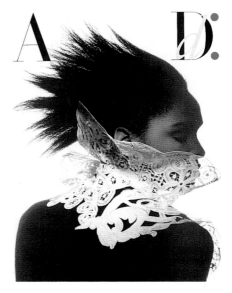

PUBLISHER
CASA DE IDÉIAS
ART DIRECTOR
**OSWALDO MIRANDA
(MIRAN)**
DESIGNER
**OSWALDO MIRANDA
(MIRAN)**
PHOTOGRAPHERS
**STEVEN KLEIN
JEAN LUTTENS
LUCIA NAPACHANN
TYEN**
LETTERING
MIRAN

By Tyen

"As Vigorosas Imagens de Tyen Para a Kodak"

PUBLISHER
CASA DE IDÉIAS
ART DIRECTOR
**OSWALDO MIRANDA
(MIRAN)**
DESIGNER
**OSWALDO MIRANDA
(MIRAN)**
PHOTOGRAPHERS
**ADC JAPAN
MITSUO KATSUI
KAZUMI KURIGAMI
MATTHEW ROLSTON
TYEN**
ILLUSTRATOR
MITSUO KATSUI

New Type

Applied Typography Japan

Tókyo

TDC

1 2 3 4 5 6 7

7 Pictures/7 Imagens Editoriais/ 7 Pictures/7 Imagens

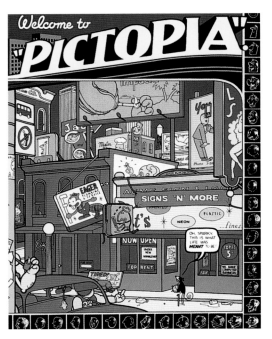

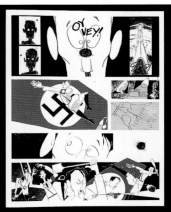

PUBLISHER
**FANTAGRAPHICS
BOOKS, INC.**
ART DIRECTOR
DALE YARGER
DESIGNERS
**PAT MORIARTY
DALE YARGER**
ILLUSTRATORS
**STEVE CASINO
KIM DEITCH
TED JOUFLAS
MARK KALESNIKO
CHRIS WARE**

USA

PICTOPIA

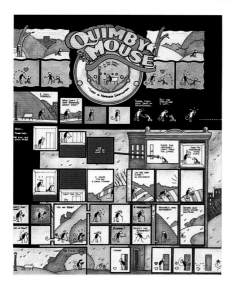

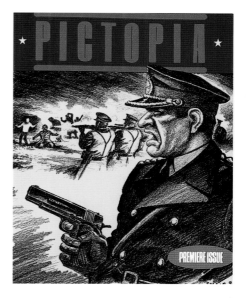

PUBLISHER
**FANTAGRAPHICS
BOOKS, INC.**
ART DIRECTOR
DALE YARGER
DESIGNERS
**PAT MORIARTY
DALE YARGER**
ILLUSTRATORS
**KIM DEITCH
TED JOUFLAS
SOLANO LOPEZ
CHRIS WARE**

JUST THE TITLE shivers the timbers. *Pictopia*: it sounds like a world devoted to images, an environment where the picture is supreme and the artist is master of his surround — could it be utopia or dystopia? In this case it is simply a magazine offering a wide range of comics and articles devoted to various methods of story telling. Slightly larger than life — or, at least, larger than most other comics magazines, *Pictopia* is firmly rooted in the "adult alternative comics" genre, a descendent of underground comics, born of the groundbreaking *Raw* magazine. But this is no meager copycat. *Pictopia*'s graphic persona is based on its careful attention to pacing, so that the varied comic styles do not form a chaotic melange. The editor's vision is also underscored by the way the table of contents and artist biographies are designed to reflect the material and define the magazine. Each cover is an original work of art and the logos are also newly designed by those artists. No two issues are the same, but spiritual consistency reigns.

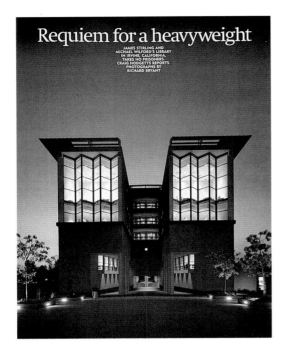

Requiem for a heavyweight

JAMES STIRLING AND
MICHAEL WILFORD'S LIBRARY
IN IRVINE, CALIFORNIA,
TAKES NO PRISONERS.
CRAIG HODGETTS REPORTS.
PHOTOGRAPHS BY
RICHARD BRYANT

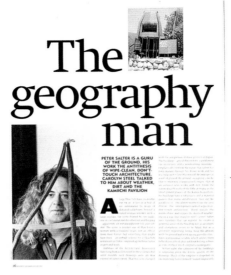

The geography man

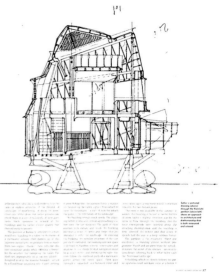

PETER SALTER IS A GURU
OF THE GROUND, HIS
WORK THE ANTITHESIS
OF WIPE-CLEAN, DON'T-
TOUCH ARCHITECTURE.
CAROLYN STEEL TALKED
TO HIM ABOUT WEATHER,
DIRT AND THE
KAMIICHI PAVILION

City of angles

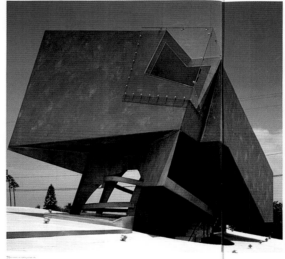

A ONCE BLIGHTED
INDUSTRIAL ZONE IN
GREATER LOS ANGELES
HAS BEEN TURNED INTO
A HABITABLE CREATIVE
HUB. MICHAEL WEBB
LOOKS AT ERIC MOSS'S
LATEST WORK AT CULVER
CITY. PHOTOGRAPHS
BY TOM BONNER

ARCHITECTURE AND DESIGN   DECEMBER/JANUARY 1995

blueprint

Opera and art

Brooks and Arad in Tel Aviv

Vanessa on shopping
Design calms down
Stirling in the sun
Peter Salter
builds

Furniture writ large

RON ARAD HAS MOVED FROM CHAIRS TO A CULTURAL
MONUMENT WITH HIS AND ALISON BROOKS'
FOYER FOR THE TEL AVIV OPERA HOUSE. ROWAN
MOORE REVIEWS THE OUTCOME

PUBLISHER
**WORDSEARCH
PUBLISHING, INC.**
ART DIRECTOR
JOHN BELKNAP
DESIGNER
JOHN BELKNAP
PHOTOGRAPHERS
TOM BONNER
RICHARD BRYANT
GADI DAGON
JAMES HUNKIN
MANN & MAN
SHOUICHI UCHIYAMA
ILLUSTRATOR
PETER SALTER

BLUEPRINT

AFTER TEN YEARS of publishing a full-color magazine in large tabloid format, *Blueprint* decided to trade in its recognizable equity — which had influenced other art and architecture periodicals — for a more experimental aura. The designer's challenge was to continue the legacy of the magazine and visually express enthusiasm for design. At the same time, the magazine also wanted to reach what its designer terms "younger, more radical designers and architects who experiment with rough edges...." In this sense the logo was redesigned as a "rougher type." The large pictures and bold use of type was "worth keeping," but more trendy effects — such as overlapping images and layered type — were avoided because they would become quickly dated. The interior is relatively restrained, allowing the subject matter — architectural photographs, product shots, and preliminary — to dominate. The size was reduced to conform to the standard British magazine shelf.

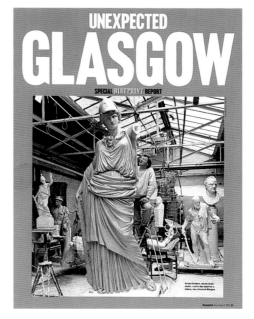

PUBLISHER
WORDSEARCH PUBLISHING, INC.
ART DIRECTOR
JOHN BELKNAP
DESIGNER
JOHN BELKNAP
PHOTOGRAPHERS
SIMON ARCHER
M. ANNE DICK
DAVID EUSTACE
ILLUSTRATOR
ANDREW KINGHAM

PUBLISHERS
ASHLEY CRAWFORD
G+B ARTS
INTERNATIONAL
ART DIRECTOR
TERENCE HOGAN
DESIGNER
TERENCE HOGAN
EDITOR-IN-CHIEF
ASHLEY CRAWFORD
PHOTOGRAPHER
MARTIN KANTOR
ILLUSTRATOR
CHARLES BURNS
DIGITAL GRAPHICS
SCOTT BENHAM

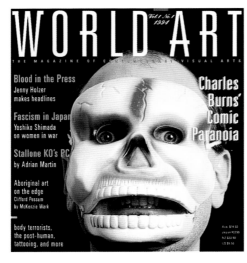

AUSTRALIA

WORLD ART

"RESPOND TO THE ART itself," is how the designer of *World Art* defines the magazine's design philosophy. It is also the sign of a prudent designer. Why impose contradictory aesthetics when a neutral presence not only enhances the subject, but also defines the magazine itself? *World Art*'s "sympathetic context" is a blend of contemporary typography and personal vision. The text is never presented in such a nondescript way as to totally eliminate the designer's self-confident hand, but the overall structure is indeed a framing device that supports the variety of art displayed within. *World Art* is designed for contemporary art aficionados, not devoted scholars or intellectuals. It is written and edited for the intelligent reader without an over reliance on theory or jargon. Its design is the visual equivalent, void of the clichés and tropes that tend to exclude, but replete with visual entry points that invite the reader to engage with the material and the magazine as a whole.

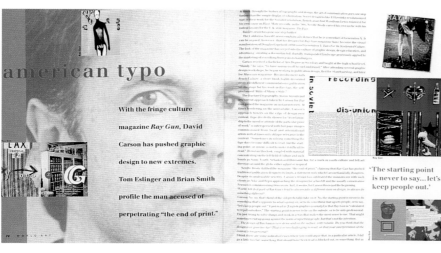

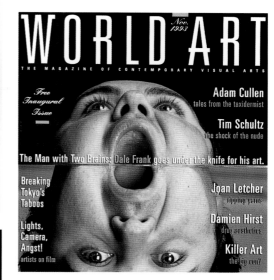

PUBLISHERS
ASHLEY CRAWFORD
G+B ARTS INTERNATIONAL
ART DIRECTOR
TERENCE HOGAN
DESIGNER
TERENCE HOGAN
EDITOR-IN-CHIEF
ASHLEY CRAWFORD
PHOTOGRAPHERS
PITO COLLAS
MARTIN KANTOR
ANDREW STACEY
ILLUSTRATOR
JON McCORMACK

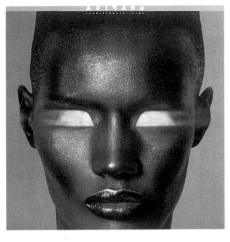

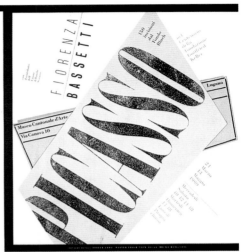

PUBLISHER
CASA DE IDÉIAS
ART DIRECTOR
**OSWALDO MIRANDA
(MIRAN)**
DESIGNER
**OSWALDO MIRANDA
(MIRAN)**
PHOTOGRAPHERS
**JEAN PAUL GOUDE
KLAUS MITELLDORF
BRUNO MONGUZZI**
ILLUSTRATOR
BRAD HOLLAND

BRAZIL GRÁFICA

PUBLISHER
CASA DE IDÉIAS
ART DIRECTOR
OSWALDO MIRANDA (MIRAN)
DESIGNER
OSWALDO MIRANDA (MIRAN)
PHOTOGRAPHER
BOB WOLFENSON
ILLUSTRATORS
ERIC DINNYER
ALAIN LE FOUL
SAUL STEINBERG
PHOTO/ILLUSTRATOR
ERIC DINNYER

THIS GLOSSY GRAPHIC design showcase of the most exemplary international work balances the integrity of the diverse material featured with an unmistakable overall design persona. The designer's penchant for "retro" typography cut with a contemporary hand does not interfere with the featured collection of modern, eclectic, and post-modern design methodologies, and yet it perfectly frames everything. The articles are portfolios; a strong graphic opening spread introduces the featured designer or design process with minimal text that may flow onto one or two additional pages. The rest of the feature section is comprised of freestanding imagery with discretely placed captions. Although the magazine is totally designed to evoke a particular visual point of view, the subject matter can be viewed on its own merit. The large, square format contributes to *Gráfica*'s personality; its cover is a full-bleed image (usually a detail from work shown inside) with the logo band stretching along the top — coverlines are rejected. Its full-color interior on glossy paperstock makes this a superb environment for the reproduction of good design.

Silent partner

I am still feeling well enough to stoutly maintain against all critics (including my son) that I have more brains, common sense and know how generally than any two engineers civil or uncivil that I have ever met and but for me the **Brooklyn Bridge** would never have the name **Roebling** in any way connected with it. —Emy Roebling

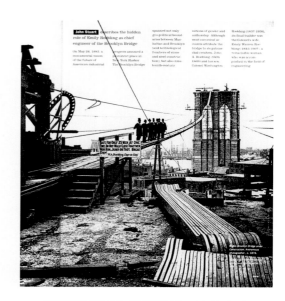

CANADA

A|R|C

FOR AN ACADEMIC publication which addresses interdisciplinary concerns within architecture and the built environment in terms of society, economics, and politics, *A|R|C*'s design format is resolutely accessible to a broader audience. Although the text is aimed at professionals, scholars, and design students, the "neutral and clean" format, as the designers themselves describe it, is actually quite inviting to anyone with an interest in this subject matter. The design certainly reflects the content, and does not dictate or impose a fashionable style. All text pages are one or two colors, while the covers are three. Since there is literally no art budget, all the visuals are "found" or supplied by the firms and institutions covered. The covers are the most expressive of the magazine, but *A|R|C* is a fine example of how with limited means a magazine can be given a memorable personality.

Social Housing:

technology of power

or architecture of

social possibility

PUBLISHER
**ATLAS OF THE
CITY PUBLICATIONS**
ART DIRECTOR
ARTHUR NIEMI
DESIGNERS
**MARK KOUDYS
ARTHUR NIEMI
ALISON UPPER**
ARTIST
**ADOLPHE WILLIAM BOUGUEREAU/
CHRISTIE'S OF LONDON
CRANACH**

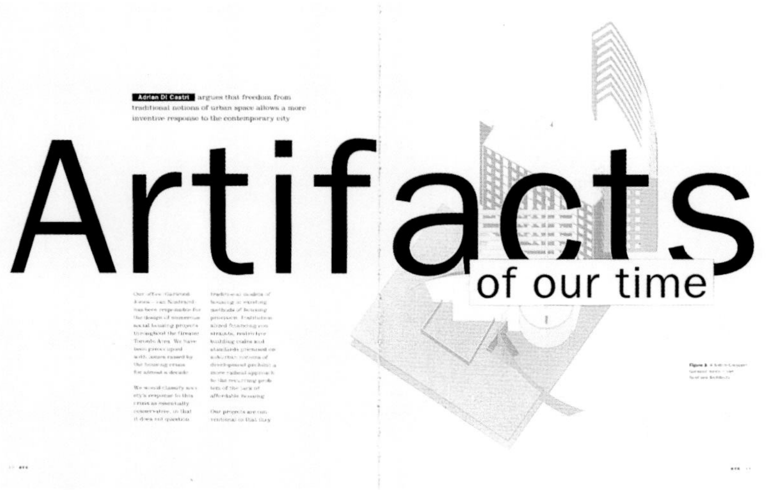
Adrian Di Castri argues that freedom from traditional notions of urban space allows a more inventive response to the contemporary city

Artifacts

of our time

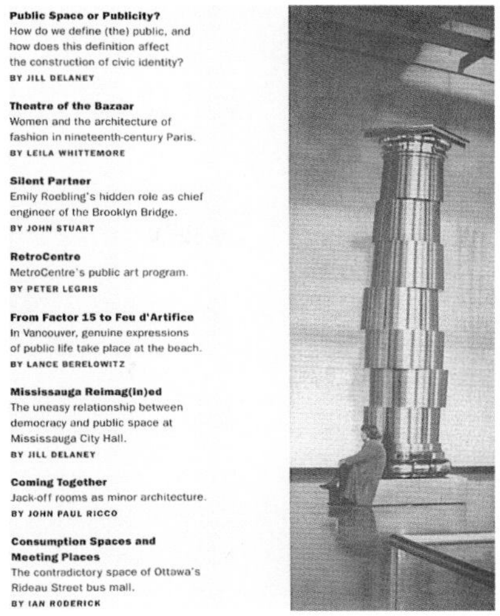
Public Space or Publicity?
How do we define (the) public, and how does this definition affect the construction of civic identity?
BY JILL DELANEY

Theatre of the Bazaar
Women and the architecture of fashion in nineteenth-century Paris.
BY LEILA WHITTEMORE

Silent Partner
Emily Roebling's hidden role as chief engineer of the Brooklyn Bridge.
BY JOHN STUART

RetroCentre
MetroCentre's public art program.
BY PETER LEGRIS

From Factor 15 to Feu d'Artifice
In Vancouver, genuine expressions of public life take place at the beach.
BY LANCE BERELOWITZ

Mississauga Reimag(in)ed
The uneasy relationship between democracy and public space at Mississauga City Hall.
BY JILL DELANEY

Coming Together
Jack-off rooms as minor architecture.
BY JOHN PAUL RICCO

Consumption Spaces and Meeting Places
The contradictory space of Ottawa's Rideau Street bus mall.
BY IAN RODERICK

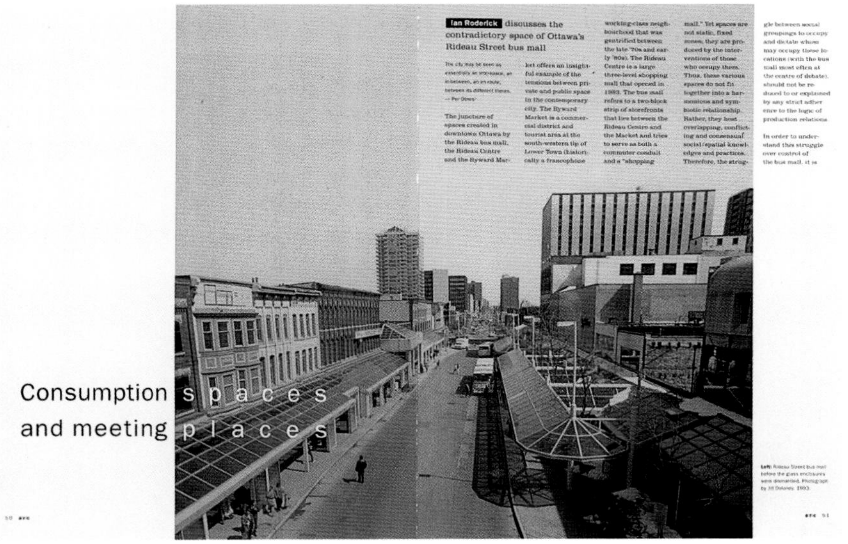
Ian Roderick discusses the contradictory space of Ottawa's Rideau Street bus mall

Consumption spaces
and meeting places

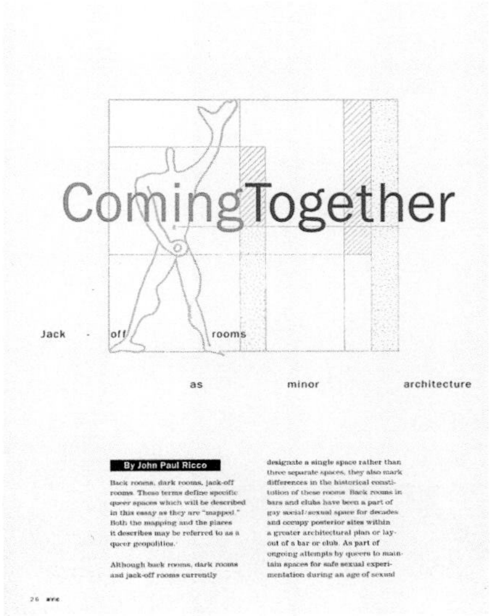
ComingTogether

Jack - off rooms as minor architecture

By John Paul Ricco

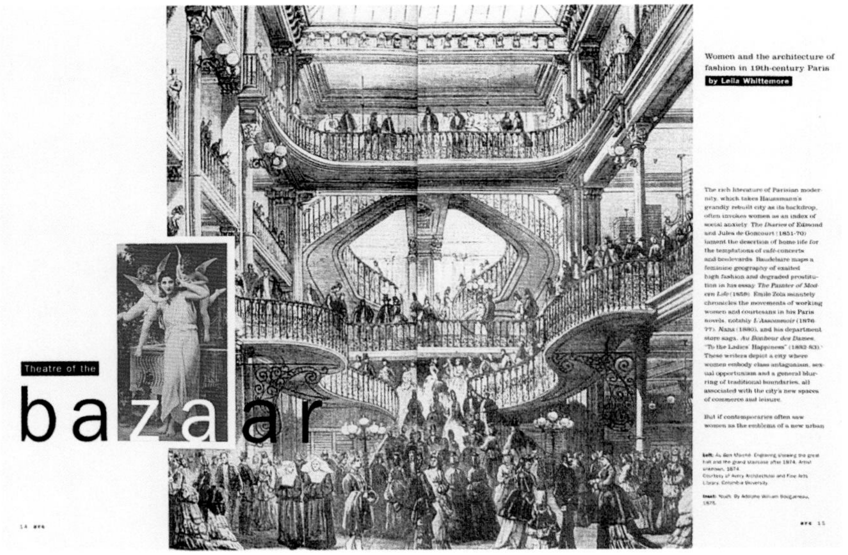
Women and the architecture of fashion in 19th-century Paris
by Leila Whittemore

Theatre of the
bazaar

PUBLISHER
ATLAS OF THE CITY PUBLICATIONS
ART DIRECTOR
ARTHUR NIEMI
DESIGNERS
MARK KOUDYS
ARTHUR NIEMI
ALISON UPPER
ARTISTS
ADOLPHE WILLIAM BOUGUEREAU/ CHRISTIE'S OF LONDON
CRANACH
PHOTOGRAPHER
JILL DELANEY
ILLUSTRATION
GARWOOD-JONES & VAN NOSTRAND ARCHITECTS

CANADA

C MAGAZINE

LOW BUDGET IS THE CURSE of most
contemporary art magazines, but it is
also the spark that ignites the engine of
invention. *C Magazine*, a forum for art
and ideas that surround art, attempts to
overcome the fiscal restraints in a variety
of ways. *C*'s covers, for example, are
striking crops of unusual artworks, often
printed in full color and topped by the
iconic, lone *C* as the masthead. The interior is black and white printed with what
the designer says are "special combinations of inks to produce deep, rich blacks
on high quality tactile paper." The typography often transcends the conventions
of mainstream art journals, but is not so
quirky as to be either self-conscious or
illegible. In addition a key feature of *C*'s
editorial and design personality is the
"artists' pages" dedicated to selected
contemporary artists as a kind of tabula
rasa. Although overseen by the editor
and designer, these oases in a more rigid
editorial envelope add a degree of
serendipity to the magazine.

PUBLISHER
**C ARTS PUBLISHING &
PRODUCTION, INC.**
ART DIRECTORS
**CLAUDE MARTEL
SUSAN McCALLUM**
DESIGNERS
**CLAUDE MARTEL
SUSAN McCALLUM**
ARTISTS
**PIERRE DORION
LAUREN SCHAFFER**
PHOTOGRAPHERS
**MARION BRYSON
LOUIS LUSSIER
CHRISTOPHER McNAMARA
CARLA WOLF/ VIDEO OUT
DISTRIBUTION**
ILLUSTRATORS
**CHRISTOPHER McNAMARA
CARLA WOLF**

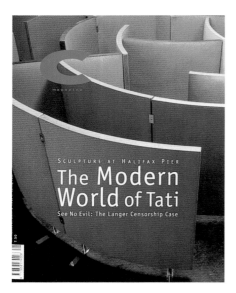
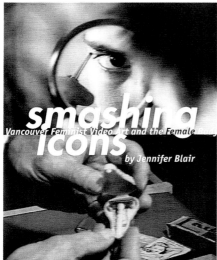
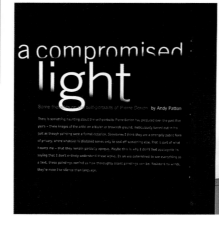

(again)

plus Pierre Dorion, Murray Favro, transgressions at the EAG, reviews & reports

the sublime is now

7.50
contemporary art quarterly · issue 64 winter 1999

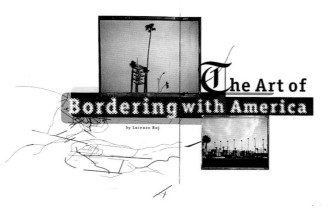

The Art of Bordering with America

by Lorenzo Buj

PUBLISHER
**C ARTS PUBLISHING &
PRODUCTION, INC.**
ART DIRECTORS
**CLAUDE MARTEL
SUSAN McCALLUM**
DESIGNERS
**CLAUDE MARTEL
SUSAN McCALLUM**
ARTISTS
**JIMMIE DURHAM
ANDY PATTON
LAUREN SCHAFFER**
PHOTOGRAPHERS
**ISAAC APPLEBAUM
MARION BRYSON
NICOLE KLAGSBRUN GALLERY
CHRISTOPHER McNAMARA
JACQUES TATI/
CEPEC/ PANORAMIC**
ILLUSTRATOR
INGRID REEHILL

now

the sublime is

Ghosts

Sculpture Photographed at Halifax

Pier 21

by Robin Peck

Design Delirium

The Films of

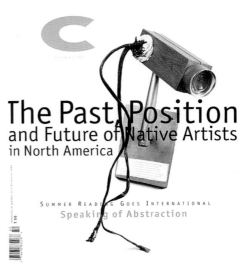

The Past, Position
and Future of Native Artists
in North America

SUMMER READING GOES INTERNATIONAL
Speaking of Abstraction

ISSUE TWO $12

BLIND SPOT
PHOTOGRAPHY

DAVID BYRNE
JAMES CASEBERE
GREGORY CREWDSON
WILLIAM EGGELSTON
ANDREA MODICA
JACK PIERSON
FRANK SCHRAM
VICTOR SHRAGER
JOEL-PETER WITKIN
THOMAS STRUTH
HIROSHI SUGIMOTO

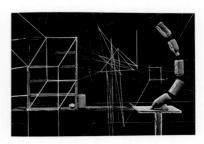

ISSUE THREE $12

BLIND SPOT
PHOTOGRAPHY

JOHN BALDESSARI
ZEKE BERMAN
CHRISTIAN BOLTANSKI
PETER CAMPUS
PATRICK FAIGENBAUM
LEE FRIEDLANDER
DAVID LEVINTHAL
SALLY MANN
DUANE MICHALS
RUTH THORNE-THOMSEN

PUBLISHER
**KIM ZORN CAPUTO/
LEXINGTON LABS**
DESIGNER
TONY AREFIN
PHOTOGRAPHERS
**ZEKE BERMAN
CHRISTIAN BOLTANSKI
JAMES CASEBER
SUSAN DERGES
VICTOR SHRAGER
BRUCE WEBER**

ISSUE FOUR $12

BLIND SPOT

PHOTOGRAPHY

LYNN DAVIS
JOAN FONCUBERTA
ROBERT FRANK
ADAM FÜSS
DAVID HILLIARD
MARY ELLEN MARK
BEVERLY SEMMES
JEFF WALL
BOYD WEBB
BRUCE WEBER

Bruce Weber

Gentle Giants

USA

BLIND SPOT

IT SEEMS THAT PHOTOGRAPHY magazines compete less for readers than vie for which magazine will be the most exquisitely produced and designed. *Blind Spot* holds it own in this category. Its first notable achievement is an elegant patina of rotogravure printing on an offset press which makes the photographs appear like original prints. Secondly, *Blind Spot* is a perfect balance between text and picture. The articles are not lengthy critical discourses but introductions to the artists' method and work. Typography is readable, and effectively serves as a framing device for what the designer calls "close focus" pictures which are arranged as if on a gallery wall — juxtaposed with an emphasis on scale and proportion. Its high-quality paper and dominant black color give *Blind Spot* the feel of a fine art book rather than a magazine, and in an age where magazines are increasingly more cluttered with image and type it is refreshing to find, and perhaps courageous to provide, a magazine that refrains from indulging in contemporary tropes.

PUBLISHER
GRAPHIS US, INC.
ART DIRECTORS
GREG HOM
B. MARTIN PEDERSEN
DESIGNER
B. MARTIN PEDERSEN
GREG HOM
PHOTOGRAPHERS
DONNATELLA BLUM
MICHAEL FURMAN
ADAM SAVITCH

SWITZERLAND

GRAPHIS

SINCE 1947 *GRAPHIS* HAS been the premier international graphic design magazine, and for much of that time it maintained a strict "Swiss" format. For the past ten years, under a new publisher, it has changed its appearance several times. At first, it attempted to define itself in relation to both the past and the contemporary design environment; in recent years, however, it has found both its editorial niche and visual personality. *Graphis* is the most lavish showcase of international talent published today; everything about the magazine — from its posterlike cover to its typography — is designed to be lush and exuberent. The cover (for subscribers) is a striking image with a courageously discrete, liliputian logo in a band along the left side, while the newsstand cover loudly sells the magazine's contents with bold coverlines that surprint over the image.

Inside, every spread is a distinctive portfolio introduced by an elegantly bold text and picture combination. Full-page photographs of the designer(s) are shot exclusively for the magazine, and the best still lifes are used to display their designs. *Graphis* is not only about total design, but its own design is totally controlled, leaving nothing to chance.

(By Chloé Braunstein-Dance Photo by Adam Savitch)

The Birth of a Typographer The path followed by designer Philippe Apeloig owes much to chance events—to random encounters, and to the respect and staunch loyalty he has granted those who chose to place their trust in him. Apeloig writes as well as he draws, and takes pride in exercising his profession

50

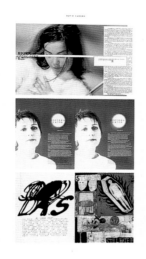

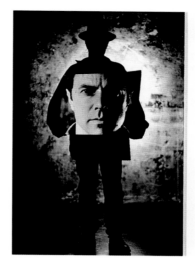

The Wunderkind of Design As David Carson breaks all the rules, he reinforces their importance. The rock music magazine RAY GUN, with its fractured layouts and tortured typography, has for the past two years served as a sort of Rorschach test within the graphic design world: Where some see brilliance and innovation, others see

PUBLISHER
GRAPHIS US, INC.
ART DIRECTOR
B. MARTIN PEDERSEN
DESIGNERS
DAVID CARSON
B. MARTIN PEDERSEN
POST-TOOL DESIGN
PHOTOGRAPHERS
ART BREWER
RICHARD CALDICOTT
AARON CHANG
CHRIS CUFFARRO
JOANNE DUGAN
LOURDES LEGORRETA
MARY SCANION
TOM SERVAIS
PETE WARD
DIGITAL COMPOSITOR
WICHAR JIEMPREECHA

ture is." When the history of Mexican architecture is written, one man will be said to have designed it from the inside out. Ricardo Legorreta,

the grande maestro of Mexico's architectural establishment who reportedly crashed a party thrown for Walter Gropius so he might obtain

INTERIOR DESIGN OUTLOOK

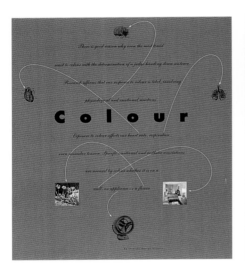

PUBLISHER
**ASSOCIATION OF
REGISTERED INTERIOR
DESIGNERS OF ONTARIO**
ART DIRECTOR
DEBBIE ADAMS
DESIGNER
CHRISTOPHER CAMPBELL
PAINTING
**THE CANADIANA DEPART-
MENT/ROYAL ONTARIO
MUSEUM**
PHOTOGRAPHER
ADAMS + ASSOCIATES

OPULENT PROFESSIONS often have professional organizations that produce opulent-looking trade journals. Considering that interior design is one of the more upscale professions and supports a wealth of consumer magazines, it is admirable that the journal of Canadian registered interior designers is tightly budgeted, yet beautifully produced. Member supported, *Interior Design Outlook* does not enjoy large advertising revenues to support full-color, glossy extravaganzas, but its designers do a brilliant job of compensating with fine typography and imaginative visuals. The use of original photography and illustration is confined to a very few special projects, but the average reader would never perceive that the majority of images used are handouts or pickups. Variation in scale is used to add dimension and accentuate and differentiate visual material. Curiously, the journal is sheet-fed printed, which allows for better quality control than a web press, but confines full color only to those forms with color advertising; the rest of the book is one or two colors. The challenges have focused the designers on doing the best with the least, and *Interior Design Outlook* is a testament to working within limited means.

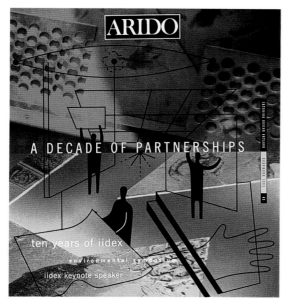

A DECADE OF PARTNERSHIPS

ten years of iidex

environmental symposium

iidex keynote speaker

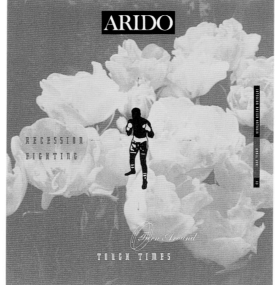

RECESSION FIGHTING

Turn Around

TOUGH TIMES

PUBLISHER
ASSOCIATION OF REGISTERED INTERIOR DESIGNERS OF ONTARIO
ART DIRECTOR
DEBBIE ADAMS
DESIGNER
CHRISTOPHER CAMPBELL
PHOTOGRAPHER
ADAMS + ASSOCIATES
ILLUSTRATOR
DOUG ROSS

Colour

TRENDS

GOING GLOBAL

GST and the Bigger Picture

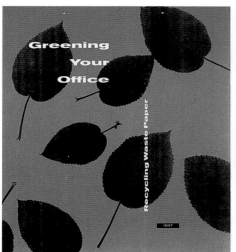

Greening Your Office

Recycling Waste Paper

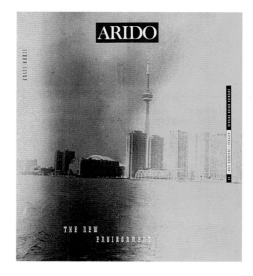

THE NEW ENVIRONMENT

ART ISSUES.

THERE ARE FEW MORE difficult assignments than to make a text-heavy journal inviting, except perhaps to design a text-heavy art magazine as excitingly as possible without losing a sense of either its literacy or its visual purpose. *Art Issues.* accomplishes this by rejecting any "glossy" or "slick" tendencies in favor of an economical two-color approach. Pictures play second fiddle to the text, but nevertheless this is not stolid in any way. Its editor boasts that *Art Issues.* is the only serious contemporary art magazine west of the Mississippi with an international reputation." And while the articles are the meat of its success, the distinctive design certainly offers a warmer invitation to the reader than most academic journals.

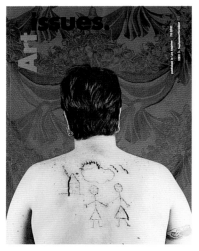

PUBLISHER
THE FOUNDATION FOR ADVANCED CRITICAL STUDIES
DESIGNERS
LINDA NORLEN SHIFFMAN/YOUNG DESIGN GROUP
ARTISTS
BRUCE OF LOS ANGELES GILAH YELIN HIRSCH CATHY OPIE RUBÉN ORTÍS-TORRES TOM OTTERNESS

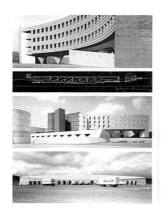

ANY

ARCHITECTURE NEW YORK is a tabloid magazine of theory and criticism, directed "to an audience of well-informed and cutting-edge readers," say its editors. Everything about this magazine is bigger than average, and to an extent larger than life. While maintaining a strict typographic "architecture" the images are allowed air to grow and breathe. In fact, although the typography does not vary from issue to issue, changing scale in relation to the images and the overall size of the publication keep it exciting and moving. Another important feature is the economy of both paper and color. No fancy coated stock and glitzy color printing to make this a monument to artifice, ANY is a functional journal devoted to functional art in which aesthetic concerns are paramount. During this image-oriented era when even many low-budget magazines have resorted to pyrotechnics to attract attention, ANY adheres to the Modern dicta that less is more, and God is in the details.

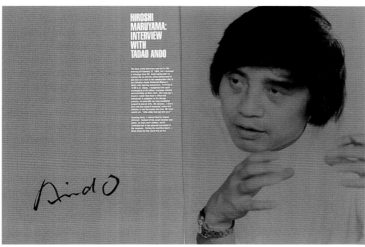

PUBLISHER
ANYONE CORPORATION
ART DIRECTOR
MASSIMO VIGNELLI
DESIGNERS
JUDY GEIB
MASSIMO VIGNELLI
ARTISTS
EDWARD CLODD/LOUVRE
MUSEUM
DAVID DIRNGER/SYMBOL
TECHNOLOGIES
PHOTOGRAPHERS
RICHARD BRYANT/ARCAID
J. STERLING
ILLUSTRATOR
TADAO ANDO/RAIKA

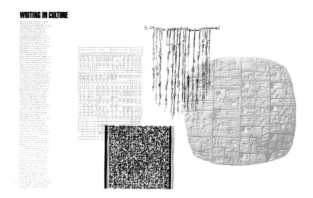

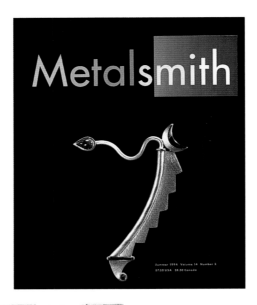

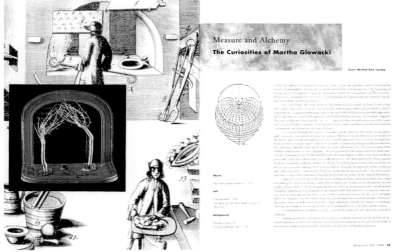

PUBLISHER
**SOCIETY OF NORTH
AMERICAN GOLDSMITHS**
DESIGN DIRECTOR
RICHARD MEHL
ART DIRECTORS
**RICHARD MEHL
MARY MELILLI**
DESIGNERS
**RICHARD MEHL
MARY MELILLI**
ARTISTS
**CHERYL RYDMARK
KIFF SLEMMONS**
PHOTOGRAPHERS
**MARTHA GLOWACKI
CHERYL RYDMARK
ROD SLEMMONS**

USA

METALSMITH

THERE ARE MANY MAGAZINES devoted to American arts and crafts but few are as visually exciting as *Metalsmith*, a magazine for metalsmithing and jewelry-making. Originally, as the *Goldsmith Journal*, it had a somewhat lackluster format, which required "modifying the visual voice," as the designer calls it, "without making drastic design or format changes." This was successfully accomplished by standardizing the typography — Futura and Garamond — and simplifying the way the pages were structured. The result is an envelope that contains visual excitement. Every issue includes a variety of images and, since all the pictures are supplied by the artists or galleries, a broad range of image quality. Scale is a tool that nets surprisingly alluring spreads and allows both the good- and poor-quality images to sit side by side without looking amateurish. All art objects and jewelry are shown not on or near a body, but in a "neutral manner," such as in a still life, that "encourages an intense critique of the form." Another important design consideration is the extended, or deep, editorial well of uninterrupted pages, which allows the designer to deliberately pace the visual flow as if a film on paper.

American Indian shaman and Enid necklace
Photo by Alida Latham

Enid Kaplan, *Fertility Amulet*, 1992
14k, sterling, copper, shell,
carnelian, gold leaf, 6 x 1½ x 1"
(Amulet for creativity,
abundance, fertility, expression)
Photo by Todd Flasher

Lisa Norton

 Objects for Inscribing a Vernacular History

by Michal Ann Carley

M onumentality

in

miniature

The
Narrative Jewelry of
Robin Kranitsky
and Kim Overstreet

by Gail M. Brown

Metalsmith

Fall 1992
VOLUME 12
NUMBER 4
87

PUBLISHER
**SOCIETY OF NORTH
AMERICAN GOLDSMITHS**
DESIGN DIRECTOR
RICHARD MEHL
ART DIRECTORS
**RICHARD MEHL
MARY MELILLI**
DESIGNERS
**RICHARD MEHL
MARY MELILLI**
ARTISTS
**ENID KAPLAN
ROBIN KRANITSKY
LISA NORTON
KIM OVERSTREET**
PHOTOGRAPHERS
**TODD FLASHER
ALIDA LATHAM
LISA NORTON
JACK RAMSDALE**

I GIGANTI DELLA PRATERIA

PUBLISHER
**EDITRICE ABITARE
SEGESTA**
ART DIRECTOR
ARCH. ITALO LUPI
ARTISTS
**GUIDO
SCARABOTTOLO
SAUL STEINBERG**
PHOTOGRAPHERS
**GIANNI BERENGO
GARDIN
TONI NICOLINI**
ILLUSTRATOR
GEORGE HARDIE

LE PARETI DEGLI ILLUSTRATORI

"FORSE POSSEDENDO GLI OGGETTI DA BAMBINI NOI CREDIAMO DI POSSEDERE IL MONDO STESSO"

Il desiderio dell'accumulo, quasi una forma di furore per Guarnaccia e il limpido nitore della parete di Lionni. La scansione del tempo (solo letterario?) che ghita lo studio di Periccoli. I legni "narranti-sette-man" che arridano la vita di Guidotti. Gli immancabili omaggi a Piero che scaldano come falò mediterranei l'algida casa di Glaser. Tutto questo può essere racchiuso tra due concetti. Il primo venne annotato da Henry Lartigue nel suo diario: "Forse possedendo gli oggetti da bambini noi crediamo di possedere il mondo stesso". Il secondo fu scritto da Giuseppe Ungaretti in forma di poesia: "Il vero Michelangelo che murava / tutti gli spazi in un baleno / non concedendo all'anima / nemmeno il privilegio / di spezzarsi". Trovata una nostra bussola, bussiamo e visitiamo. ■ The desire to hoard, in Guarnaccia a manic almost, in Lionni the clear brightness of a wall; in Periccoli's studio, a scansion of time that seems more than literary; in Guidotti's life, driftwood and detritus that "speaks of the seven seas"; in Glaser's icy home, unfailing tributes to Piero della Francesca that warm the air like bonfires lit on Mediterranean shores. Various situations but two basic concepts, the first in Henry Lartigue's diary - "Perhaps the objects we possess as children make us believe we possess the world itself" - the second in Giuseppe Ungaretti's verse - "Michelangelo, tense and intent, walling in space in the winking of an eye, sparing not even his soul's birthright of heart's ache and break". Having found our bearings, let us now knock and enter to see what awaits us.

ABITARE
A
321

Lire 10.000
Prezzo
in Italia

$ 11.50
Europe
Overseas

CASE DOVE
SI PUO
LAVORARE
HOMES YOU CAN WORK IN

CASE DOVE
SI DEVE
LAVORARE
HOMES YOU HAVE TO WORK IN

ARCHITETTURE
PER IL LAVORO
WORKPLACE ARCHITECTURE

DESIGN
E PRODUZIONE
PER L'UFFICIO:
TELEFONI,
SEDIE, COMPUTER,
LAMPADE, FAX,
POLTRONE,
SCRIVANIE
DESIGN & PRODUCTS FOR THE OFFICE

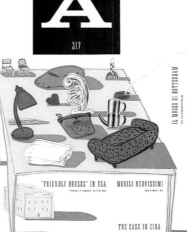

ABITARE
A
317

Lire 10.000
Prezzo
in Italia

$ 11.60
Europe
Overseas

DESIGN ANONIMO E DESIGN SPONTANEO

BIANCONI: IL DISEGNO COME PASSIONE

IL MUSEO DI ROTTERDAM

"FRIENDLY HOUSES" IN USA

MOBILI NUOVISSIMI

TRE CASE IN CINA

ABITARE

ALTHOUGH *ABITARE* COVERS fashionable design and architectural fashions in the home and office, its own design is not slavishly fashionable; rather it exudes a classic contemporaneity — late-twentieth-century Modernism at its foremost, with a touch of wit and pinch of humor. Its feature well, defined by superb interior and architectural photography and smart conceptual illustration, is sandwiched between a front and back of the book consisting of columns, news and listings, all designed with an eye towards the accessible and functional. Nevertheless, *Abitare* does not lack a unique identity. Usually illustrated with a symbolic drawing or painting against a few discrete coverlines, its cover sets the tone with a clean design and generous white space. In addition *Abitare* overcomes a difficult design problem — publishing in two languages, Italian and English — without losing overall graphic impact.

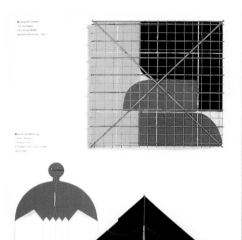

PUBLISHER
**EDITRICE ABITARE
SEGESTA**
ART DIRECTOR
ARCH. ITALO LUPI
ARTISTS
**SHIGKRU JUFUKU
LEO LIONNI
ALBERTO PIOVANO
SAUL STEINBERG**

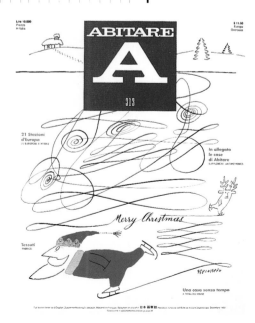

THE BOSTON GLOBE MAGAZINE
DIALOGUE
EL MUNDO MAGAZINE
GLOBAL

NEWS & BUSINESS

LOTUS QUARTERLY
THE NEW YORK TIMES MAGAZINE
REGIONAL REVIEW
THE WASHINGTON POST MAGAZINE
WORLD TOUR

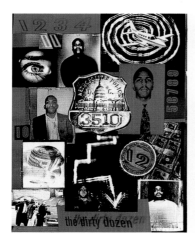

Anatomy Of a Sting

THE FASTEST GUITAR IN THE EAST — OR THE WEST, OR THE SOUTH— OR ANYWHERE ON THE PLANET, REALLY. A LOT OF PEOPLE THINK DANNY GATTON IS THE BEST GUITAR PLAYER ALIVE. SO WHY DO FAME AND FORTUNE JUST KEEP STRINGING HIM ALONG? BY RICHARD HARRINGTON

When Henry Met Zsa Zsa

PUBLISHER
THE WASHINGTON POST COMPANY
ART DIRECTORS
RICHARD BAKER
KELLY DOE
DESIGNER
KELLY DOE
PHOTOGRAPHERS
NANCY ANDREWS
AMY GUIP
MARK HANAUER
CLAUDE VAZQUEZ
KENNARD WILLARDT
MICHAEL WILLIAMSON
ILLUSTRATORS
DAVID HUGHES
LANE SMITH

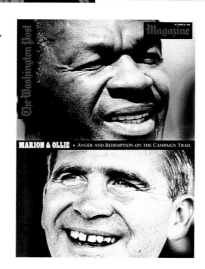

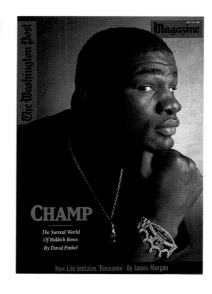

USA

THE WASHINGTON POST MAGAZINE

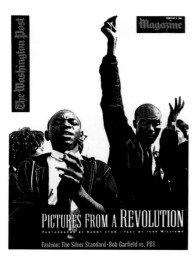

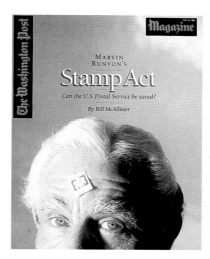

PUBLISHER
THE WASHINGTON POST COMPANY
ART DIRECTOR
KELLY DOE
DESIGNER
KELLY DOE
PHOTOGRAPHERS
RUSSELL KAYE
DANNY LYON/MAGNUM
BRIAN SMALE
ILLUSTRATOR
C.F. PAYNE

ACCORDING TO ITS EDITOR, *The Washington Post Magazine* is the only magazine of its size, a narrow 8''x 10½'' with a constant 32 pages — the only magazine that people can put in their back pockets. This dubious distinction has actually been the largest design challenge. "We attempt to create a visual sensibility that is bold enough to compensate for our size," says the designer. But like the proverbial David, this magazine packs a wallop of graphic impact. From its distinctive cover logo treatment — *The Washington Post* masthead goes up the left side in a box, while the lone, unpretentious boxed word *Magazine* sits horizontally at the upper right — to the bold picture/text openers inside, design is not marginalized. Within this decidedly visual environment, the images are totally editorial — each telling a particular story or conveying a pointed message. The cover for "Stamp Act," a photograph of the postmaster general from the nose up, with a postage stamp stuck on his forehead, is a simple, delightfully comic way to treat this government analysis. Indeed the gift of *The Washington Post Magazine* is its alluring presentation of the commonplace or mundane using extraordinary graphics.

PUBLISHER
**DUN & BRADSTREET
SOFTWARE**
ART DIRECTOR
GARY KOEPKE
DESIGN
KOEPKE INT'L, LTD.
PHOTOGRAPHER
UPI/BETTMAN
ILLUSTRATORS
**GREETINGS FROM
"THE VOYAGER TIME
CAPSULES"**

USA

WORLD TOUR

IF ONE DID NOT KNOW that this was a business magazine it might be mistaken for an experimental typography or graphics journal. Although there are actually a limited number of rather conventional typefaces used, they are treated with a devil-may-care playfulness. Single words and phrases set in large and small gothics emphasize editorial points of view. Like the words, the images are bites of information composed to give the reader immediate signposts, in contrast to more conceptual illustrations that require some code deciphering. *World Tour*'s covers set the tone; all are pure typography (or letterforms) with terse word bites, like the interior typographic scheme. The covers are also limited to two colors — red in the logo and black, a conscious echo of the Russian Constructivist palette, and one of the most eye-catching combinations in today's color-saturated print environment. The tabloid format and uncoated calendared paperstock further adds to the streetwise quality of this design.

WoRld ToUR

A REVIEW OF BUSINESS AND TECHNOLOGY NEWS PUBLISHED BY DUN & BRADSTREET SOFTWARE   VOLUME 3 NO 2   JULY–SEPTEMBER 1993

can you

TAKE THE HEAT

PUBLISHER
DUN & BRADSTREET SOFTWARE
ART DIRECTOR
GARY KOEPKE
DESIGNERS
KOEPKE INT'L, LTD.
PHOTOGRAPHERS
ANTON BRUEHL
JEFF KOONS
ILLUSTRATORS
BASIL VALENTINE'S WILL AND TESTAMENT
GRAY'S ANATOMY
GREETINGS FROM "THE VOYAGER TIME CAPSULES"

manage

biotech

virtue

cooperate

competence

The Norwegian explorer Roald Amundsen was the first to reach the South Pole on December 11, 1911. His management style was based on meticulous planning and a choice of capable men to whom he gave almost absolute freedom of operation. One pilot said that Amundsen's ship was the most astonishing he'd ever seen: "No orders were given, but everyone seemed to know exactly what to do." Amundsen's chief rival in the race to the pole was the Englishman Robert Scott. Scott reached the pole a month after Amundsen did and lost his life and the lives of his men on their return.

WT10

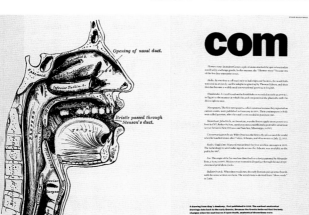

Opening of nasal duct.

Bristle passed through Stenson's duct.

com

RUSSIA

duplicity

The term *Parthian shot*—meaning parting shot—alludes to the warlike horsemen of Parthia (now northeast Iran), who turned their horses and seemed to flee in terror. Those foolish enough to pursue died in a hail of arrows as the horsemen suddenly fired over their shoulders.

bad

worse

Russian pay phones only accept 15-kopek coins. Recognizing a seller's market, entrepreneurs are hoarding the coins to drive up the price. NEWSWEEK, MARCH 22

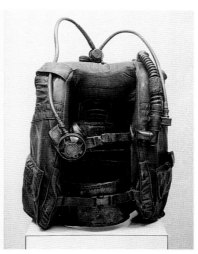

Jeff Koons, Snorkel Vest, 1985.

WT 138

threat

hope

challenge

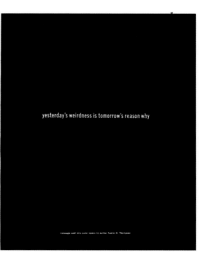

yesterday's weirdness is tomorrow's reason why

THE NEW YORK TIMES MAGAZINE

HERE IS ANOTHER VENERABLE institution which over the past couple of decades has undergone various redesigns and reformats. The current redesign which was launched in 1993 had the distinction of reducing all the magazine's display type to variants of one family, Cheltenham, a traditional news face for *The New York Times*. What at first seemed to be a confining typographic palette has become a creative boon. While it forces the magazine's designers to address the ins and outs of only one family, it also gives them great freedom to complement it in countless ways. The type color, size, and scale, for example, can be as variegated as possible. But it can also be used as a neutral frame for explosive illustration, poignant photography, and any other visual stimulation. Sandwiched between a front and back of the book, the editorial well contains a very long story and various shorter ones — including visual features and photojournalist essays, which regardless of the typographic consistency are always remarkably different. The back of the book fashion section is a mini-republic all its own, comprised of some of the most exciting (imaginative and entertaining) photographic layouts in any Sunday newspaper supplement published today.

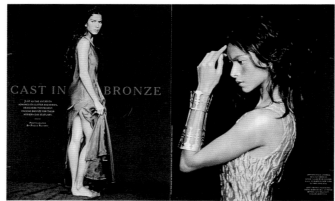

PUBLISHER
**THE NEW YORK
TIMES CO.**
ART DIRECTOR
JANET FROELICH
DESIGNERS
NANCY HARRIS
PETRA MERCKER
JAMIE OLIVERI
PHOTOGRAPHERS
DONNA FERRATO
PAOLO ROVERSI
SEBASTIÃO SALGADO

The New York Times Magazine

BERLIN MUST LOOK LIKE BERLIN

BUT WHAT DOES THAT MEAN?
REBUILDING THE CAPITAL OF EUROPE
BY PAUL GOLDBERGER

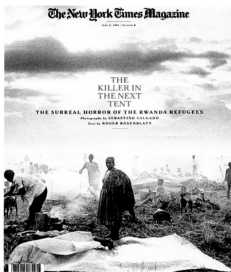

The New York Times Magazine

THE
KILLER IN
THE NEXT
TENT

THE SURREAL HORROR OF THE RWANDA REFUGEES

Photographs by SEBASTIÃO SALGADO
Text by ROGER ROSENBLATT

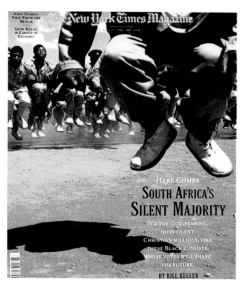

The New York Times Magazine

HERE COMES
SOUTH AFRICA'S
SILENT MAJORITY

It's the GOD-FEARING,
NONVIOLENT
CHRISTIAN MILLIONS, LIKE
THESE BLACK ZIONISTS,
WHOSE VOTES WILL SHAPE
THE FUTURE.

BY BILL KELLER

THE SOUND OF COSSACK THUNDER

The fearsome horsemen of a violent Russian past are back, teaching a new generation to fight for God and country.

HOW TO GIVE
ORDERS
LIKE A MAN

BY DEBORAH TANNEN

ART DIRECTOR
JANET FROELICH
DESIGNERS
JOEL CUYLER
GINA DAVIS
JANET FROELICH
CATHY GILMORE-BARNES
NANCY HARRIS
PHOTOGRAPHERS
ELLEN BINDER
JAMES NACHTWEY/
MAGNUM
JEFFREY NEWBURY
KATHY RYAN (PHOTO EDITING)
SEBASTIÃO SALGADO
ALBERT WATSON
ILLUSTRATOR
GARY BASEMAN

The New York Times Magazine

FROM MY WIFE'S ROOM
By Robert Kotlowitz
A JACKPOT FOR CHILDREN
LIAM NEESON'S FLASHES OF ANGER

The Black Man
Is in Terrible Trouble.
Whose Problem
Is That?

A round-table discussion
with Patrick Day, Ken Hamblin,
Joseph Marshall, Hugh Price,
John Singleton and
William Julius Wilson,
moderated by Bob Herbert.

ANOTHER
DAY AT
THE BORDER

In Rwanda this summer,
variations of life
in the mass production
of death.

PHOTOGRAPHS BY JAMES NACHTWEY
TEXT BY JIM WOOTEN

Capturing a Corner of the World

Afri-Cola's strategies against Coke and Pepsi are a lesson in niche marketing

by Dana Bartlett

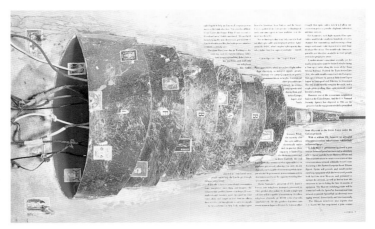

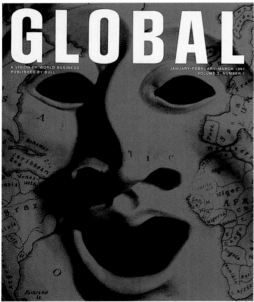

GLOBAL

A VISION OF WORLD BUSINESS
PUBLISHED BY BULL

JANUARY·FEBRUARY·MARCH 1991
VOLUME 2, NUMBER 1

The Decline of Communism

As the computer revolution unleashed the
creative power, initiative, and talent of individuals,
democracy was no longer an option for
Eastern Europe; it was a must

by Silviu Brucan

GLOBAL

A VISION OF WORLD BUSINESS

MARCH 1990 PREMIER ISSUE

PUBLISHER
BULL H.N. INFORMATION SYSTEMS, INC.
ART DIRECTOR
GARY KOEPKE
DESIGNER
LISA LAARMAN
PHOTOGRAPHERS
STEVE MARSEL
HANS NELEMAN
ILLUSTRATORS
HENRIK DRESCHER
ANITA KUNZ
BARBARA NESSIM

Virtual Reality

It will revolutionize work and play in the 21st Century,
but its effects will be felt long before then

By Christopher Morgan

USA

GLOBAL

PUBLISHER
**BULL H.N. INFORMATION
SYSTEMS, INC.**
ART DIRECTOR
GARY KOEPKE
DESIGNER
LISA LAARMAN
PHOTOGRAPHERS
**JOEL LEVINSON
HANS NELEMAN**
ILLUSTRATOR
IAN BECK

THIS LARGE-SCALE, full-color journal
of business news is the envy of any
designer. Without advertising, the editorial well has unrestricted flow allowing for
well-balanced pacing. *Global*'s covers are
mini-posters unencumbered by coverlines, and its interior layouts are the perfect balance of text and image (with
slightly more emphasis on image). Excellent conceptual illustrators are given full-
color, often full-page opportunities to
interpret a wide range of business
themes. The typography frames the
images, but also defines the publication's visual persona. Trendy faces are
rejected in favor of handsome cuts of
both classic and Modern faces. The text
faces are a bit light, and sometimes
appear more as texture than reading
matter. Nevertheless, a reader should
have no trouble navigating since every
element is meticulously placed both to
avoid confusion and provide an elegance
that most business journals avoid.

PUBLISHER
NORBORD INDUSTRIES
ART DIRECTORS
MICHAEL CHERKAS
ARTHUR NIEMI
DESIGNER
MICHAEL CHERKAS
PHOTOGRAPHERS
COLIN ERRICSON
ROBERT KARPA
EDEN ROBBINS
BRIAN SMALE

CANADA

DIALOGUE

HERE IS AN EXAMPLE of a company newsletter transformed from an ugly duckling into a beautiful swan. The metaphor may be old, but *Dialogue* is among the freshest, most exciting "in-house" magazines published today. Originally a four-page, two-color mailer, its designer was charged with the task of improving its design and production values while remaining within a strict budget. Editorial changes—expanding the scope to include company profiles and product news of interest to its workers and customers—sparked the robust design scheme. Printing four-over-one gives the illusion of a full-color magazine at half the cost. The cover was the first to be remade, with the main photography supplemented by an inserted detail and captioned, so to speak, by the logo on the bottom rather than top of the page. The interior picks up the cover motif, with a standard typeface and a strictly gridded scheme for laying out photographs. Having full-bleed and double-truck images gives the impression of a vast editorial well. There are, however, relatively few design variations — the conceptual weight is on the photography — which makes laying this out a rather simple procedure.

LAKE ABITIBI, A SHALLOW
lake 150 kilometres
long and 100 kilometres
wide, straddles the
Ontario/Quebec border
(Below.) Early in this
century, the Catholic
church, in vogue with
the provincial govern-
ment, encouraged
Quebecois to settle in
the Abitibi region
by giving land away.

La Sarre *A pioneer town with*
an investment in the future.
photography by BERNARD BOHN

WHEN 93-YEAR-OLD ERNEST TRUDEL AND HIS FIVE BROTHERS ARRIVED in La Sarre, Quebec 77 years ago, it was their father's idea. His rea-soning was simple: The economy had stalled badly. Jobs were scarce in southern Quebec. And he couldn't give each son enough land to make a proper farm. But land was cheap in those days if you went north. Dirt cheap. In La Sarre, which is 650 kilometres northwest of Mon-treal and about the same distance south of James Bay, the price was

---

The town of Cochrane, Ontario
has experienced change for over 80 years developing a unique
spirit of community in the process

NORTHERN

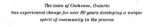

EXPOSURE

In the Cochrane Railway and Pioneer Museum curator Paul Latondress has a favourite photograph. It's a posed photo from about 1910, the year of the town's incor-poration. All the town-people are convened in front of the first building

in the centre of town on 6th Ave. All the people, but none of the women, Laton-dress observes. "To the best of our know-ledge, they were all cook-ing up lunch for the men" Latondress says. Sixth Ave still runs through the centre of town, but much

BY RICHARD WRIGHT
PHOTOGRAPHY BY EDEN ROBBINS

The polar bear greets all visitors to the town of Cochrane, the starting point for the Polar Bear Express that travels the scenic railroute north to James Bay, and most polar bears.

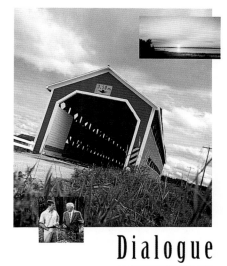

Dialogue

A River Runs Through It
Even before the arrival of Norbord MDF, forest products played a central role in the history of Deposit, New York

"Where nature blesses, there man progresses", became Deposit's motto in the early 1950s. It seemed then, as it does to-day, an appropriate description of the small rur-al community nestled in the foothills of New York's Catskill Mountains. Strategically located on the Delaware River and accessible by rail and highway, Deposit seemed assured both per-manence and prosperity as a transportation hub for the region. Incorporated in 1811, the town grew up with the lumber industry. For over 100 years the most important and lucrative business along the Delaware River was in

norbord

Did you lock out?

Your life depends on it!

Dialogue

PUBLISHER
NORBORD INDUSTRIES
ART DIRECTORS
MICHAEL CHERKAS
ARTHUR NIEMI
DESIGNER
MICHAEL CHERKAS
PHOTOGRAPHERS
BERNARD BOHN
EVAN DION
DWAYNE LOBDELL
DEPOSIT HISTORICAL
SOCIETY
EDEN ROBBINS

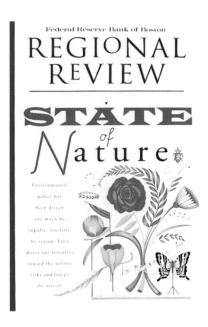

USA

REGIONAL REVIEW

ECONOMICS — ESPECIALLY when explained by bankers, investment analysts, and academics — can be as deadly as a cannonball, and as heavy. The idea behind *Regional Review*, a roundup of economy and business research, was to defuse the bomb with handsome design and witty illustration. The shape of the cover contributes to this accessibility — the long narrow format invites a kind of playbill aesthetic. Indeed the logo, set in a handsome roman, is classic and serious, but when set against the more eclectic cover headlines and impressionistic drawings, the overall tone is lightened. Interior spreads are equally sprightly. The text is widely leaded with generous amounts of white margin space. Large initial caps add boldness to the pages, while pastel-colored illustrations provide a conceptual counterpoint to the articles. The headline types contribute a poster-like quality to each page. Despite the serious nature of the magazine, the designer plays with the forms while maintaining a strict identity.

PUBLISHER
**FEDERAL RESERVE BANK
OF BOSTON**
ART DIRECTOR
RONN CAMPISI
DESIGNER
RONN CAMPISI
ILLUSTRATORS
SETH JABEN
JEAN TUTTLE
JOE VAN DER BOS
ELLEN WEINSTEIN

PUBLISHER
**FEDERAL RESERVE BANK
OF BOSTON**
ART DIRECTOR
RONN CAMPISI
DESIGNER
RONN CAMPISI
ILLUSTRATORS
**MICHAEL BARTALOS
DIANE BIGDA
MARIS BISHOFS
DAVID DIAZ
ROBERT PIZZO
JAMES STEINBERG**

By Steven Sass

HOW MUCH
is that
BUILDING
in the
WINDOW?

The boom and bust in New England office building values

Enormous

INVESTING IN THE FRONT LINE
OR
The New Art of Cutting Metal

By John Campbell

CRISIS
in Pensions

By Steven Sass

E MPLOYER PENSIONS, long considered a pillar of the nation's old-age income system, slipped during the 1980s. The proportion of the work force enrolled in these programs dropped precipitously, and the prospect of gaining an adequate pension grew chancier. Meanwhile, employer-based savings plans — profit sharing, employee stock ownership, stock bonus, and 401(k)-type programs — mushroomed up in the decade. These plans

issues in finance

Interest in the Future

P

Spreads between securities of different maturity have little predictive value.

RIGHTING
the SCALES
➤ The search for balance in health care

By Norman Boucher
and Jane Little

| The Making of Practical Economics |

Economic
FORECASTING

By Leslie Brunetta

E CONOMISTS WOULD SEEM TO BE the natural ally of business and government. Economists study production, prices, employment, wages   the practical world in which business and government operate. The statistics, insights, and especially the predictions offered by economists would seem critical

Familiarity has bred contempt for the doctrine, but also complete acceptance of the practice.

EL MUNDO MAGAZINE

THIS SUPPLEMENT FOR the Spanish daily *El Mundo* faced two challenges: to equal its parent newspaper's visual vitality and originality, and to blaze new trails in the field of supplement design which has been qualitatively high in Europe. *El Mundo Magazine* has risen to the occasion. It is a splendid example of eclectic typography wed to strong photography, with just the right balance between editorial and visual weight. And yet for the American viewer there is a nagging sense of déjà vu: what *El Mundo* does so very well, is echo the aesthetics of *Rolling Stone*. From its outline, slab serif logo that says *Magazine* as if it were a poster, to the reliance on adapted nineteenth-century types and typecase-like gridded layouts, there is a profound sense of *Rolling Stone*'s aesthetic and formal presence. Now this would be rather unfortunate if it was not done well — and it is — or if the ideas were borrowed without the benefit of interpretation — which it is not. *El Mundo Magazine* definitely has its own personality in the photographs and illustrations that run throughout each issue of this weekly magazine.

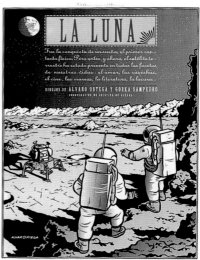

PUBLISHER
UNIDAD EDITORIAL S.A.
DESIGN DIRECTOR
CARMELO CADEROT
ART DIRECTORS
MIGUEL BUCKENMEYER
RODRIGO SANCHEZ
PHOTOGRAPHERS
NASA
RAGHU RAI
ILLUSTRATOR
ALVARO ORTEGA

PUBLISHER
UNIDAD EDITORIAL S.A.
DESIGN DIRECTOR
CARMELO CADEROT
ART DIRECTORS
MIGUEL BUCKENMEYER
RODRIGO SANCHEZ
PHOTOGRAPHERS
FELIPE ALONSO
DANIEL GIRY
CARLOS MIRALLES
BEGOÑA RIUAS
ILLUSTRATOR
RAÚL ARIAS

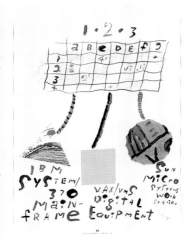

PUBLISHER
**LOTUS DEVELOPMENT
CORPORATION**
ART DIRECTOR
RONN CAMPISI
DESIGNER
RONN CAMPISI
ILLUSTRATORS
**JAMES ENDICOTT
MARK FISHER
LILLA ROGERS**

LOTUS QUARTERLY

GIVING INFORMATION on technology an inviting format is not as easy as it might seem. *Lotus Quarterly*, published for Lotus's customers, has to be accessible but at the same time authoritative. Colorful conceptual drawings used on the covers and most interior spreads build the magazine's persona — mostly a type of lighthearted, surrealistic style. A limited number of classic types are used, with an emphasis on large initial caps which echo the large black *Q* on the cover. This provides a visual focal point, but also forces the designer to capitalize letters that are not always cozy fits with the rest of the headline. The large-scale initials work best when only one is used on a page, usually as the lead of a paragraph; two or more suggest a type catalog rather than an editorial introduction. Nevertheless, this method results in a strong identity for the *Quarterly* which is both inviting and friendly.

Short takes

LOTUSWORKS

Integrated Software for Entry-Level Users

LOTUS NOTES

Alliance Partners Add Value for Customers

Volume III Number 4 Fall 1990

LOTUS QUARTERLY

LOTUS HAS TAKEN
THE SPREADSHEET TO
THE NEXT LEVEL...
Introducing Improv

Volume II Number 1 Fall 1989

LOTUS QUARTERLY

**Lotus 1-2-3
Release 2.2**
It's like a new set
of wheels

Interview:
David Roux
spins CD products to
global heights

DataLens:
Going
beyond file
importing
and exporting

Lotus @Work

Agenda
proves an advantage for the
DISADVANTAGED

**TRW Improves
Opportunities for
Minority Vendors**

JONE EL FAYE REMEMBERS the way it was under the old system. She's librarian of the vendors database for the Space and Technology Group (S&TG) of TRW Inc., a major defense contractor. The database catalogs more than 1,000 suppliers of everything from screws to semi-conductors and when S&TG buyers put together a bid proposal for a government contract, they call on it for the "whats, hows and whos" of meeting the contract specs. Or, more accurately, they call on El Faye for the information. And for her, it used to be quite a challenge. "The old database management

Lotus @ Work

THE NUMBERS ARE IN

1-2-3 Release 2.2
Means
Insurance FOR
The Travelers

IT'S HARD TO THINK OF the insurance business and the game of baseball in the same context, but these two very different activities have one thing in common both are numbers-crazy. Just as baseball fans are eager to know, say, how many times a particular ballplayer has gone zero-for-three at

Grill 23 &
Bar

COOKIN'
WITH
1 - 2 - 3

It's a hot, still summer evening in Boston's historic Back Bay district, but it's cool and airy inside Grill 23 & Bar, an elegant restaurant housed in the building that used to serve as Salada Tea's headquarters. Under the high ceiling held up by Greek pillars, people sip vintage wines and feast on prime aged sirloin steaks, grilled salmon and swordfish, prime rib, veal and lamb chops. ¶ In a city with many superb European restaurants, Grill 23 stands out

PUBLISHER
**LOTUS DEVELOPMENT
CORPORATION**
ART DIRECTOR/DESIGNER
RONN CAMPISI
ILLUSTRATORS
**PHILIP ANDERSON
POLLY BECKER
FRITZ DUMVILLE
CATHI FELSTEAD
TIM LEWIS
JEAN TUTTLE**

PUBLISHER

THE BOSTON GLOBE

ART DIRECTOR

LUCY BARTHOLOMAY

DESIGNER

LUCY BARTHOLOMAY

PHOTOGRAPHER

STAN GROSSFELD

ILLUSTRATORS

TERRY ALLEN

MARY ANNE ERICKSON

MALCOLM TARLOFSKY

ARTIST

LEONARDO DA VINCI

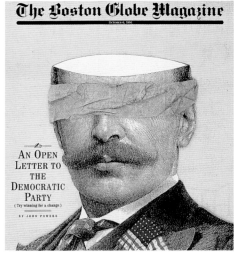

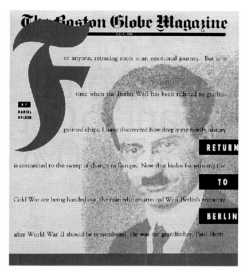

THE BOSTON GLOBE MAGAZINE

USA

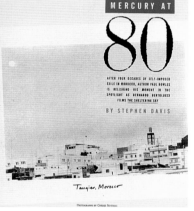

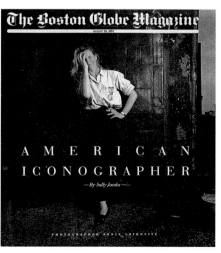

PUBLISHER
THE BOSTON GLOBE
ART DIRECTOR
LUCY BARTHOLOMAY
DESIGNER
LUCY BARTHOLOMAY
PHOTOGRAPHERS
YUNGHI KIM
ANNIE LEIBOVITZ
CHERIE NUTTING
ILLUSTRATOR
BRIAN CRONIN

SINCE THE 1980s this has been the epitome of Sunday newspaper supplement design. Where once such publications were rooted in newspaper makeup, the *Globe Magazine* was a distinctive hybrid between news and magazine. When it was first redesigned, new ways of using blurbs, applying white space, and building visual interest on strong imagery were introduced. It continues to explore ways of expressing visual ideas through typography — often entire pages and spreads are built totally on manipulated letterforms. But its greatest strength is the intelligent integration of image and text. Much emphasis is put on editorial illustration, which is well-framed and conceptually positioned to give the reader a visual hit that introduces the article and keeps it flowing. Without suggesting superficiality, owing to the generous white space, there is a breezy feeling to *The Boston Globe Magazine* that beckons the reader to engage in the often excellent editorial content.

Greetings from FLORIDA "The Land of Sunshine"

BIG
ESQUIRE
FYI
HEALTH
L'AMATEUR DE BORDEAUX
L'AMATEUR DE CIGARE

LIFESTYLE

MANHATTAN FILE
MARTHA STEWART LIVING
SAVEUR
SOUTH BEACH
TENNESSEE ILLUSTRATED

chairs

From the Renaissance to the fifties, a glossary of seating

Some people never sit down. But they probably have a favorite chair or two just the same. "I can find nothing better designed for surveying the human body than eighteenth-century French chairs," says couture fashion designer Karl Lagerfeld. "Their character is so easy to read. They do with the conversations they must have heard in their youth." We revere our chairs because they become part of the family. Shouldn't we get to know them a little better? The seating time line on the following pages presents examples of twelve basic Western chair styles, each an archetype of form, materials, and decoration. Below each chair we list the full name of its type. Because chairs are probably the most common furniture form, their evolution is a valuable guide to decorative styles in general. By familiarizing yourself with the basic look of a period, you'll be better able to put any piece of furniture into its historical context. Period originals like the chairs pictured here may not cross your path every day, but you will begin to notice countless creative offspring. In chair design, reproduction has always been the sincerest form of flattery.

TEXT BY SARAH MEDFORD
ILLUSTRATIONS BY RODICA PRATO

paint it eggshell
Color inspiration can come from many sources, but the best, by far, is nature

TEXT BY WILLIAM L. HAMILTON

PUBLISHER
TIME INC.
ART DIRECTOR
GAEL TOWEY
DESIGNERS
LAURA HARRIGAN
ANNE JOHNSON
ERIC PIKE
GAEL TOWEY
PHOTOGRAPHERS
THIBEAULT JEANSON
VICTOR SCHRAGER
STYLISTS
STEPHEN EARLE
DARCY MILLER
HANNAH MILMAN
ILLUSTRATOR
RODICA PRATO

MARTHA STEWART LIVING

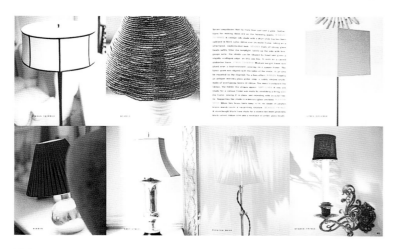

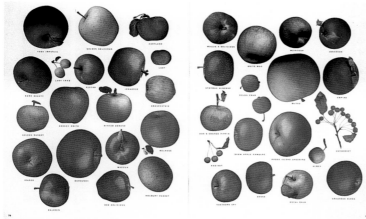

THIS IS ONE OF THE MOST popular quarterly "guide books about gardening, entertaining, cooking, and decorating" on the market today. Therefore, given the conventions of the mass marketplace one might assume that to achieve such stature the magazine must take on the "mass-market" look of cluttered covers, jigsaw puzzle layouts, and gaudy typography. Not so. *Martha Stewart Living* actually has one of the finest designs and most accessible formats. Its standards for photography have, in fact, elevated the average reader's expectations of what could be tedious how-to illustrations. Its covers are consistently geared to illustrate the seasons, and often (but not always) picture the doyen of *Living*, Martha Stewart, in the photograph. Inside, however, the reader is greeted with surprises: gorgeous spreads of apples, ferns, fall vegetables, and more are allowed to be seen and experienced unencumbered by obtrusive textblocks. Most issues seem to be designed more like a fine stylebook than a magazine. Another significant touch is the selection of a dominant color palette for each issue "so that the feeling of the season," says its design director, "is as subliminal as it is obvious."

PUBLISHER
TIME INC.
ART DIRECTOR
GAEL TOWEY
DESIGNERS
ANNE JOHNSON
GAEL TOWEY
JENNIFER WAVERICK
PHOTOGRAPHERS
RUVEN AFANADOR
DAVIES & STARR
STYLISTS
DARCY MILLER
HANNAH MILMAN

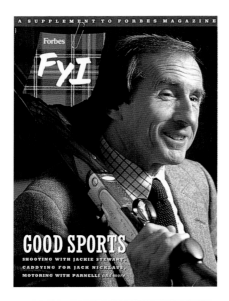

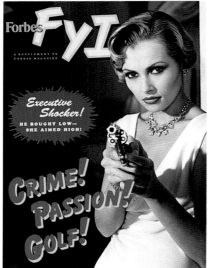

PUBLISHER
FORBES
ART DIRECTOR
ALEXANDER ISLEY
DESIGNERS
LYNETTE CORTEZ
KAY SCHUCKHART
PHOTOGRAPHERS
J. MICHAEL MYERS
NICK PASSMORE
ILLUSTRATORS
PAUL BACHEM
RONALD SEARLE

USA

FYI

THIS LIFESTYLE/SERVICE magazine for business people is a quarterly supplement, or shall we say errant younger brother, of the business bible, *Forbes* magazine. Unlike its older, more conservative sibling, *FYI* is replete with visual puns that reflect the humorous editorial tone throughout. The covers are a curious confluence of convention, pastiche, and wry wit. The logo, a hand-scrawled *FYI* (which echoes the scribbling on common memos) is often set against anomalous backgrounds (like a tartan plaid fabric swatch). Cover images are often ironic or just plain kitsch. Inside, a carnival-like table of contents with quirky illustrations introduces the controlled clutter that defines *FYI*. While body type is more or less consistent, headlines are an eclectic mix of styles and families which are manipulated for comic effect. A dot in the *i* of a golf story is actually a golf ball popping out of another letter. The *t* in a story entitled "Duct Tape" is a cross made from, you guessed it, the tape itself. With all these clever visual jokes it might appear that this was a humor magazine, but in fact, *FYI* represents the lighter side of the serious business person's agenda with charm and smarts.

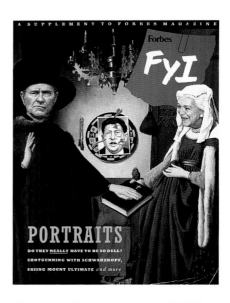

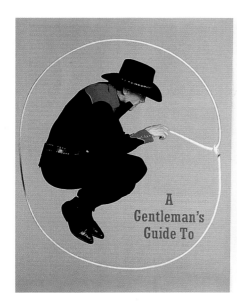

A Gentleman's Guide To

O.K., so you no longer dream that old cowboy dream

where you're holding the reins in one hand and some rope in the other, and you're riding through the dust to lasso another dogie.

Still, even as you sit at your desk, in a "saddle" designed by a Swedish ergonomist, wouldn't it feel fine to grab a lariat, toss it, and lasso your dozing assistant? (As an attention getter, it beats clearing your throat.)

And what niftier way to ward off mid-afternoon blahs than rope spinning? Master a few tricks, and the kids might even believe it when you say you once made your home on the range.

For a basic lesson in this loopy frontier art, there's no better teacher than Vince Bruce, the lanky roping wizard who's doing a star turn in the smash musical *The Will Rogers Follies*. Bruce is that rare thing—a Broadway performer who elicits genuine *oohs* and *ahs*. At the start of Act II, he holds the stage for nearly four minutes, and with a prestidigitator's deftness and dancer's grace reels off a number of dazzling rope tricks, ending with a spinning rope in each hand and (somehow) stepping through both loops—a feat never before seen (never mind described).

Bruce, who is 37, is regarded as the world's greatest rope artist, and so it comes as a surprise to meet him, for he does not speak in a Texas drawl or some other twangy Western tongue. He has a British accent. Raised on the Isle of Wight, he spun his first rope at the age of eight. Around that time, his father, an amateur roper, introduced him to the ex-patriot American roping legend Tex McLeod—a star of the 1912 Calgary Stampede—and old

Tex took the boy under his wing. By his late teens, Bruce was roping for a living, touring Europe in circuses, rodeos and Wild West shows. At the moment, he holds at least one roping record; in the Empire State Building lobby one day, he performed the Texas Skip (see opposite) 4,011 times without stopping.

Roping, you will see, is a knack thing. Doing even a simple trick is somewhat bewildering at first, but, after a number of tries, the rhythm and the flowing geometry suddenly make sense—the puzzle solves itself—and you've got it. The pleasures are unexpected. "It has a Zen quality about it," Bruce says. "You concentrate on this soothing, repetitive thing. It centers you, it's a lot like meditation."

Here then, upright gringo, are a few lassoing and spinning tips gleaned from the master.

The rope that Bruce favors is a 16-foot length of ⅜-inch-diameter cotton sash cord (preferably a brand named Sampson Spot #12). Hemp or sisal, he says, are stiff and unwieldy. And he dislikes nylon ropes—they kink.

First, tie a **honda** knot (that's Spanish, not Japanese) at one end, like this.

TIE A HONDA

Roping

BY TERENCE MONMANEY   PHOTOS BY E. H. WALLOP

Big

BIDness

BY ALLISON MOIR

"Holy Haberdashery, Batman, they're selling our costumes!"

THE ONLY WAY TO BE FIRST on the block when it comes to one-of-a-kind items is to buy at auction. So this holiday season, raise your glass—and your bidding paddles!—for some of the dazzlers from this winter's auction calendar.

Batman and Robin Costumes, Christie's East

The Dynamic Duo created in 1939 by cartoonist Bob Kane, had stints on the Superman radio show and in two movie serials in the 1940s. The campy TV show premiered in January 1966, and the Pop Art "POW!"s and "BOP!"s launched the first episode of Batman "WHAM!" into the year's top ten. Ratings went "PHHHHHT!" two years later, and the adventures of Batman (Adam West as a wooden Bruce Wayne) and Robin (Burt Ward as a goofy Dick Grayson) were canceled.

On the block is one set of the two or three original Batman and Robin costumes. The Caped Crusader's costume: a satin and castfiberglass cowl with ears, a dark blue satin cape, two-piece grey leotard with bat insignia, blue satin briefs, yellow utility belt with brass buckle and "Batman" insignia, blue satin gloves, and blue leather boots.

The Boy Wonder's costume is a bright yellow cape, red wool vest with "R" insignia, black satin and felt eye mask, green T-shirt and

Screen gem: movie posters at Christie's East.

CADDYING FOR THE BIG GUY

Hefting Jack Nicklaus's bag, **JAMES Y. BARTLETT** *has a chance to discover what makes the Golden Bear tick—and growl.*

THE 11TH HOLE AT GREAT WATERS, A NEW GOLF COURSE ON GEORGIA'S LAKE Oconee, is a short par four of just 349 yards from the back tees. The green rests diagonally on a spit of land that extends out into the lake, and it's theoretically possible, since the hole runs downhill, for big hitters to bust one down the right side, catch a favorable bounce and reach the green.

"It was interesting, in retrospect, how quickly and completely a golfer and his caddie become bound in the enterprise of golf."

Forbes FYI

A SUPPLEMENT TO FORBES MAGAZINE

NORTHERN EXPOSURES

BY SEAPLANE TO THE HEART OF ALASKA, MARTHA STEWART DOES KILIMANJARO, HEMINGWAY TAKES THE RITZ, *and more*

PUBLISHER
FORBES
ART DIRECTOR
ALEXANDER ISLEY
DESIGNERS
LYNETTE CORTEZ
PAUL DONALD
KAY SCHUCKHART
PHOTOGRAPHERS
NOËL SUTHERLAND
E. H. WALLOP
PETE WINKEL

[FYI SHOP TALK]

Duct Tape

Now and then, something comes along that is just plain undeniable. Philosophers have devised a system for classifying these things. First, there are the big things—your wheel, for instance. Or fire. And then there are your not-so-big things—the automobile and the machine gun come to mind. And then (sticking with the stricter logic of the system) you have the little things. Aspirin. Bottled (not canned) beer. wd-40.

And duct tape.

It's hard to conceive of life as we know it without duct tape. And if you could remove duct tape from modern life...well, just think of the number of things that would fall apart. We could probably get along better, for longer, as a major industrial power without the Federal Reserve System than we could without duct tape.

Aviators use duct tape to patch the skin of low-speed aircraft. In Vietnam, you measured the righteousness of a chopper by the tape on its surface. "It's perfect for expedient repairs," says one old Vietnam Forward Air Controller. "The downside is sticky as wet tar and the outside is smooth as a baby's ass."

Which is the reason mountain climbers use duct tape to cover a blister. "Works much better

than moleskin," says one. "Lots less friction."

Race car drivers use it around the body of a car to smooth things down and cut wind resistance.

There is more duct tape than chewing tobacco, these days, as the pits at Daytona. Skiers use it to bind up loose boots and patch anything that needs patching.

And the list of things that it will patch is limitless—everything from a fly rod to a laptop. About the only thing it won't patch is a broken heart.

Duct tape has even been used by fashion photographers to support the breasts of models. Honest.

Every backpacker, fishing guide, mechanic, sailor, body & fender man, and cowboy keeps a roll of duct tape handy on the sure and certain knowledge that, sooner or later, the thing you most need will break. A certain dog trainer once used duct tape as a muzzle, and it is for sure that it has been used by crooks to tie up their hostages.

But don't blame duct tape. When duct tape is banned, only criminals will have duct tape.

Duct tape is what you use to fix those things that a) you really need, b) really love, or c) cannot do without. It is scotch tape for the real world. **E**

—GEOFFREY NORMAN

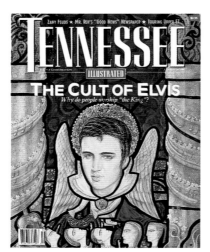

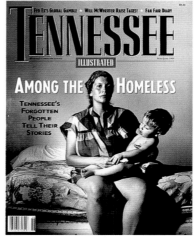

TENNESSEE ILLUSTRATED

TENNESSEE ILLUSTRATED, a regional magazine, was designed to imbue the region's character without resorting to clichés, appeal on a state-wide basis and eliminate anything that evoked the stereotypical notions of this small, but historic state. Since *Tennessee Illustrated* aimed at a general interest audience, the challenge was to maintain a visual consistency, or at least identity, while covering a wide spectrum of subjects. In fact, consistency was purposely rejected in favor of variety. The feature layouts are radically different from one to the other. Covers are likewise varied between art, photography, and typography, with conceptual approaches being the favored method.

PUBLISHER
**WHITTLE
COMMUNICATIONS**
ART DIRECTOR
MARY WORKMAN
DESIGNER
MARY WORKMAN
PHOTOGRAPHER
RUSSELL MONK
ILLUSTRATORS
**BOB PETERS
JEFFREY SMITH
JANET WOOLLEY**

G·O·O·D FolkS

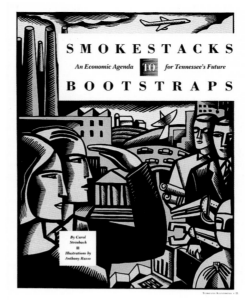

SMOKESTACKS TO BOOTSTRAPS

An Economic Agenda for Tennessee's Future

By Carol Steinbach

Illustrations by Anthony Russo

CONSCIENCE OF A COP

WRITTEN BY DAVID HUNTER
ILLUSTRATED BY BILL RUSSELL

TENNEPSYCHICS
PREDICTIONS FOR 1989

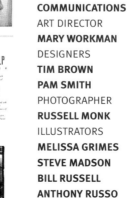

PUBLISHER
WHITTLE COMMUNICATIONS
ART DIRECTOR
MARY WORKMAN
DESIGNERS
TIM BROWN
PAM SMITH
PHOTOGRAPHER
RUSSELL MONK
ILLUSTRATORS
MELISSA GRIMES
STEVE MADSON
BILL RUSSELL
ANTHONY RUSSO

DELIVERANCE

By Vince Frost. Photographed by Giles Revell

Knock Out! Photographs by The Douglas Brothers

PUBLISHER
LOCATION PRINTING
BIG, S. L.
ART DIRECTOR
VINCE FROST
DESIGNER
VINCE FROST
PHOTOGRAPHERS
THE DOUGLAS BROTHERS
NICK KNIGHT
GILES REVELL

Big Magazine direction

88

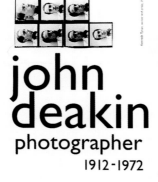

BIG

NOW HERE'S A TITLE that delivers the goods: *Big* is big on creative intelligence. From its typographic scheme to its photographic layouts, *Big* exhibits a high level of taste, imagination, and restraint; it does not blindly follow current design trends, as is the tendency of many contempo publications, but rather sets its own standard for presentation on the edge. While decidedly contemporary, *Big* recalls the late 1950s and 1960s when bold typography was used conceptually in magazines in a posterlike manner. *Big* reprises Victorian woodtypes, not as a nostalgic conceit, but to achieve graphic strength and distinction. On a spread about boxing (shown here) a stark photograph of a fighter is juxtaposed with a slab serif *KO* (knockout), in the same woodtype as would appear on an annoucement for the fight. However, here the typography is not pastiche but at once a startling graphic element and a visual pun — the *O* is indeed knocked out and on its side. In another typographic pun, the word *Deliverance*, stretching across a double page spread, is fronted by a silhouette of a hand holding up a tire iron cross. Even the covers are subtly ironic; *Big*'s hefty size and shape is a foil for the comparatively tiny logo.

PUBLISHER
LOCATION PRINTING
BIG, S. L.
ART DIRECTOR
ROBIN DERRIK
VINCE FROST
DESIGNER
VINCE FROST
PHOTOGRAPHERS
JOHN DEAKIN
THE DOUGLAS BROTHERS
ANGELA HILL

FRANCE

L'AMATEUR DE BORDEAUX

PUBLISHER
S.E.S.
ART DIRECTOR
NATA RAMPAZZO
DESIGNER
JACQUELINE HOUSSEAUX
PHOTOGRAPHERS
ANTONIO BRIGANDI
PHILIPPE HALSMAN/ MAGNUM
ISABELLE MUNOZ/ AGENCE VU
JEAN-LUC SAYEGH
JEAN VERTHEUIL

MAGAZINES FOR WINE connoisseurs must be as tasty as the vintner's essence itself. *L'Amateur de Bordeaux* certainly wets the palate with its elegant graphic style designed to put the reader at total ease with the subject. This is not a magazine where design has to compensate for difficult articles, but rather must handsomely frame what is already familiar to the reader. Indeed nothing is more satisfying to the enthusiast than a fine wine in a lovely setting, which is exactly what *L'Amateur de Bordeaux* does with its understated format and tastefully composed visuals. Included in this mix are features about the grapes, wine labels, and wines throughout the world, each illustrated in a sedate manner so as not to disturb the Zenlike experience. The covers are simple, either a still life or personality, often photographed at a distance to suggest the surroundings. Inside typography is quiet to frame the impressionistic images related to wine. Sadly, the only thing that mars the visual experience is the UPC code on the magazine cover, which on a bottle of wine is mercifully relegated to the back.

L'AMATEUR DE CIGARE

PUBLISHER
S.E.S.
ART DIRECTOR
NATA RAMPAZZO
DESIGNER
JACQUELINE HOUSSEAUX
PHOTOGRAPHERS
ESTATE BRASSAI
JOSEPH HUNWICK
TINA MERANDON

SPECIALIZED MAGAZINES have a very special problem: how to make one subject visually interesting issue after issue. *L'Amateur de Cigare* manages by combining conceptual and still-life photography with its comparatively understated typography resulting in a connoisseur's delight. Its covers show either a male or female cigar smoker savoring the moment, looking straight into the camera lens, and beckoning their peers to savor the magazine. Inside, articles on cigar smokers and cigar smoking milestones are illustrated by conceptual photography, nostalgic memorabilia, and appetizing product shots. Portfolios, such as Brassai's essay on Picasso's cigar, offer an artistic viewpoint, too. The challenge is to make a harmonious blend of the service information and the more ethereal subject matter. But *L'Amateur de Cigare* has shown its the next best thing to lighting up.

Le cigare de Picasso
par Brassaï

(Vista)

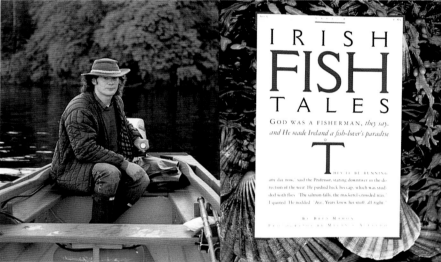

PUBLISHER
**MEIGHER
COMMUNICATIONS**
CREATIVE DIRECTOR
MICHAEL GROSSMAN
ART DIRECTORS
**JILL ARMUS
MARILU LOPEZ
PAUL ROELOFS**
DESIGNERS
**JILL ARMUS
MARILU LOPEZ
PAUL ROELOFS**
PHOTOGRAPHERS
**MELANIE ACEVEDO
CHRISTOPHER HIRSHEIMER
SAL MAIMURE/PHOTOPHILE
GEORGE MATTE/ENVISION**

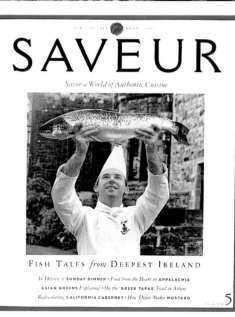

USA

SAVEUR

FOOD MAGAZINES must have an appetizing presentation. In Pavlovian fashion, readers' mouths should water merely at the sight of a page, and yet not all food magazines are so tantalizing. *Saveur*, a relative newcomer to the library of culinary periodicals, does this and more. Its food photography, a difficult art in its own right, is superb, but the reader cannot live on food pics alone. So *Saveur* covers food like a fashion magazine covers clothes and a news magazine covers world events, addressing all the details and nuances of what makes its subjects tick. In this sense *Saveur*'s visual persona encompasses the environments in which digestibles are prepared or grown or originate, and the individuals — chefs, farmers, growers — who bring such delights to the table. The magazine is bathed in a classic aura; from the covers characterized by a white margin framing an appealing photograph, to the feature openers where elegant headlines are routinely mortised out of color photographs, to the newsier "Fare" and "Kitchen" columns which smartly use sidebars, pullquotes and factoids. *Saveur* does not offer readers low-fat miracle diets, and so nor is it designed down to the mass market. This is a lovely stew of sophistication and imagination.

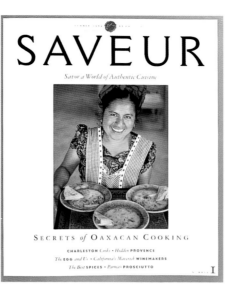

SAVEUR

Savor a World of Authentic Cuisine

SECRETS *of* OAXACAN COOKING

CHARLESTON *Cooks* • *Hidden* PROVENCE
The EGG *and Us* • *California's Maverick* WINEMAKERS
The Best SPICES • *Parma's* PROSCIUTTO

KITCHEN

Techniques and Discoveries by Our Food Editor Christopher Hirsheimer

CUTTING UP

FARE

Restaurants, Events, and Miscellaneous Morsels from the World of Food

THE TRIP OF THE ICEBERG

First grown in a Pennsylvania garden plot a century ago, this oft-maligned lettuce is now a global star

Sensuous STAR ANISE, fat rolls of China Cassia CINNAMON, rare powdered Jamaican GINGER, smoky pods of CARDAMOM, lacy Grenada MACE, Madagascar Bourbon VANILLA beans, Kashmir Mogra Cream SAFFRON from India... Sister and brother Pamela and Bill Penzey shop the wide world to bring exotic spices like these to Waukesha, Wisconsin

THE BEST LITTLE SPICE HOUSE IN AMERICA

BY ALLISON ENGEL
PHOTOGRAPHS BY
CHRISTOPHER HIRSHEIMER

FISHING CAMP COOKING

Northern Maine is hungry country, and Carol Stirling knows how to feed it—with baked beans, blueberry pancakes, and trout, trout, trout

BY CYNTHIA HACINLI • PHOTOGRAPHS BY LANGDON CLAY

PUBLISHER
MEIGHER COMMUNICATIONS
CREATIVE DIRECTOR
MICHAEL GROSSMAN
ART DIRECTORS
JILL ARMUS
MARILU LOPEZ
PAUL ROELOFS
DESIGNERS
JILL ARMUS
MARILU LOPEZ
PAUL ROELOFS
PHOTOGRAPHERS
LANGDON CLAY
FRANCIS FORD
CHRISTOPHER HIRSHEIMER
LAURIE SMITH

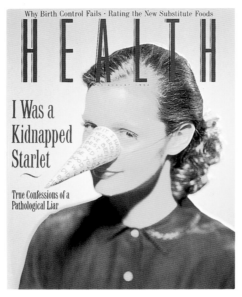

PUBLISHER
**THE HEALTH
PUBLISHING GROUP**
ART DIRECTOR
JANE PALECEK
DESIGNERS
**DOROTHY MARSCHALL
JANE PALECEK**
PHOTOGRAPHERS
**GEOF KERN
CARIN KRASNER
STEFANO MASSEI**

USA

HEALTH

EVERYONE WANTS TO have it, but rarely wants to read about good health. So the job of the designer for a magazine on nutrition, exercise, drug treatments, as well as social issues and government policy, is really to provide both the veneer and content that makes it acceptable — even stylish — to read and be concerned about health. This magazine, simply called *Health* — which as a lone word on the cover suggests "heal-eth thyself" — is smartly designed to suggest that it is as understandable (and enjoyable) as any fashion, lifestyle, or service magazine. Its covers featuring attractive women fit the mold of most contemporary magazines. Minimal coverlines focusing on one theme, such as breast cancer and low-fat diets, are revealing and to the point. The typography inside is at once eclectic and expressive. Although extremely stylized, the headlines do not force the reader to squint or decipher. Illustrations are equally conceptual, often lighthearted, and the photography is dramatic, at times quite witty. In total *Health* is a healthy mix of necessary information and visual stimulation.

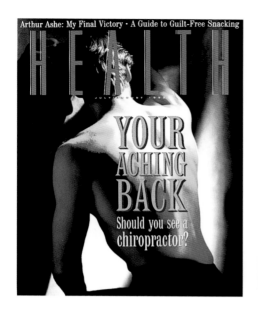

Arthur Ashe: My Final Victory · A Guide to Guilt-Free Snacking

HEALTH

JULY-AUGUST 1993

YOUR ACHING BACK

Should you see a chiropractor?

CONFESSIONS

AS A 300-POUND
UNDERCOVER AGENT,
HARRY GOSSETT FOUND
HIMSELF IN SOME
PRETTY TIGHT SITUATIONS.
BUT NOTHING SCARED
HIM LIKE STEPPING ONTO
J. EDGAR HOOVER'S
SCALE.

of a
FAT G MAN

· BY MARK KRAM ·

PHOTOGRAPHS BY BRIAN SMALE

HEALTH PLAN ROULETTE

WOULD YOU RATHER CHOOSE YOUR OWN DOCTOR
OR PAY LESS AND SKIP THE PAPERWORK?

By Paul Cuban

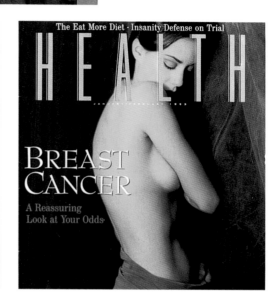

The Eat More Diet · Insanity Defense on Trial

HEALTH

JANUARY/FEBRUARY 1993

BREAST CANCER

A Reassuring
Look at Your Odds

EATING FOR LONG LIFE

THE MAN WHO HAS A BEEF WITH YOUR DIET

Harvard's Walter Willett thinks the usual warnings about fatty foods are wrong

By Michael Mason

PUBLISHER
THE HEALTH PUBLISHING GROUP
ART DIRECTOR
JANE PALECEK
DESIGNER
JANE PALECEK
PHOTOGRAPHERS
DAVID BINDER
MARK HANAUER
MARIA ROBLEDO
BRIAN SMALE
LISA SPINDLER
ILLUSTRATOR
BRIAN CRONIN

stylefile

911

Life in New York is one big emergency. Why not dress for it?

RELIGION

RELIGION

IN SEARCH OF GOD

A NEW SPIRITUALITY

Each generation has looked for answers. In the '60s, drugs promised salvation. In the '70s, the "me" generation got high on themselves while in the '80s we turned down to the blessed buck. Dimitri Ehrlich speaks with young people— within organized religion and beyond it—searching for spiritual meaning in their lives. PHOTOGRAPHS BY MARCIE IAN BRONSTEIN

PUBLISHER
**NEWS COMMUNICA-
TIONS, INC.**
EDITOR
CRISTINA GREEVEN
ART DIRECTOR
RON DE LA PENA
DESIGNER
RON DE LA PENA
PHOTOGRAPHERS
GARTH AITKINS
JUDSON BAKER
CHRISTINA LESSA
ARTISTS
RITA ACKERMAN
CHRISTIAN SCHUMANN

connections... are the issue Not connections that follow old art-world politics, criticizing and estimating artists and their works, but connections which have yet to be invented. In the past, there was a tendency to gather together certain ideas about art and the way art was to be made. Today we see there are many ways to approach art and the art-making process. This arrows the people who are viewing the art work, as well as the artist, to make up their own minds about what they see and feel in relationship to their own experiences. So, as a result, each private age creates its own image, but the way in which the image is created is increasingly growing outside the confines of what I call "the slow boxing effect." This means classifying ways of making art into categories for the convenience of history. Art is growing beyond this principle of categorization simply because artists today are not afraid to play out their own concepts of what art can and should be. Christian Schumann, Rita Ackermann, Laurel Katz, Aleen Beckman, and Andrea Zittel are five artists who present the images of contradiction that make up the world today. Produced by John Martin Newsom

BEWARE OF THE VAMPIRESS

SHE'S BEEN SIGHTED STALKING THE LOST STREETS ON THE OUTSKIRTS OF MANHATTAN IN THE PRE-DAWN HOURS. BOTH HAUNTING AND HUNTED. UNMISTAKABLY DRIVEN BY A LUST FOR LIFE. THE VAMPIRESS IS A WOMAN WHO PLAYS FOR KEEPS, A SOUL WHO SEES BEYOND THE SUPERFICIAL ASPECTS OF ORDINARY SEDUCTION AND WANTS MORE...SO STARE INTO HER EYES IF YOU DARE BUT BEWARE: SOMETIMES ETERNITY IS JUST A KISS AWAY. PHOTOGRAPHED BY GARTH AIKENS

USA
MANHATTAN FILE

THE BIGGEST challenge in producing a magazine for "young affluent New Yorkers in their twenties" is finding a niche (and the right codes) that will appeal to this totally saturated market. Not only are New Yorkers bombarded with waves of lifestyle, culture, and service publications, they are hit as well with 70 cable TV channels, posters, billboards, in short, all manner of visual stimuli. *Manhattan File*, which has targeted this frenetic group, decided that rather than try to capture them with edgy conceits they would seduce them with elegant trappings. The magazine is therefore visually rooted in the haute design of say, *Harper's Bazaar*, but with its own distinctive twist. The visual menu includes a collection of alluring fashion images, stark portraits, and a potpourri of product still lifes. The classic Bodoni is the primary typeface, supplemented by tasteful gothics in airy compositions. The second biggest challenge for *Manhattan File*, say its designers, is that owing to budget constraints most of the editorial must be printed in black and white. In fact, in a color-saturated print environment the lack of pigment and hue is a distinctive unifying touch.

PUBLISHER
**SOUTH BEACH
MAGAZINE, INC.**
ART DIRECTORS
**JAMIE FERRAND
VICTORIA MADDOCKS**
DESIGNERS
**JAMIE FERRAND
VICTORIA MADDOCKS**
PHOTOGRAPHERS
**MORRIS LAPIDUS
GALLEN MEI**
ILLUSTRATOR
ALAN E. COBER

USA
SOUTH BEACH

THE AGE WHEN GREAT American regional magazines flowered has past, but it's left a tradition that local magazines — with high and low budgets — are compelled to follow. *Southbeach* represents a small strip of land in South Florida, and consistent with the legacy of the best regionals, it is designed with quality and taste. Or as its designer boasts, "the design of the publication attempted to convey the essence of the area — light, uncomplicated, fun, glamorous, clubby, beachy, fresh...the magazine is a kind of visual vacation." While the Art Deco aesthetic of South Beach is not overtly evident in the magazine, it does have its own decorative charm. Printed on a beige paperstock (reminiscent of the beach, perhaps) the color is somewhat muted (as if in the sun too long). Covers are photographs of people and places along the strip, evoking a wish-you-were-here postcard feeling. Interior layouts are purposely subdued, with tasteful typography lending only the subtlest color to the muted page. In the feature well conceptual and mood illustrations and photographs are usually given full-bleed treatment, and provide a sharp contrast to the mellow opposite page. The contents page is also understated, and so, contributes to the all around softness of this delightful magazine.

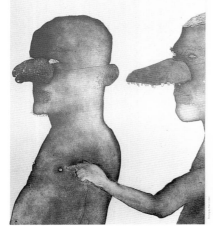

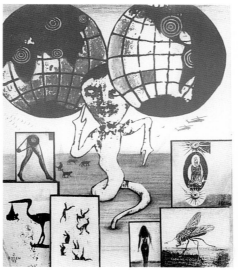

POPULATION^{rap}

Recently I had the opportunity to interview several...um...entities concerning the Earth's single biggest environmental problem: overpopulation.

It brought back to mind a cartoon I saw a few years ago. The world sits in a doctor's office, a little stick figure with a huge head with all these latitude and longitude lines. The world is trying to read a chart on the wall to test its vision. The chart has all the world's problems listed. Globe-head looks miserable.

Globe-head: I can read everything but the top line. The top line is the one with the largest print, and it says: TOO MANY PEOPLE.

Doctor (*whiner*) How many people is too many? It's over the office now. How big a number is that? A bigbigbig baseball stadium holds about fifty-thousand people...oh, right...decide later.

***

Sitting on the three prime cubicles around U.I.M.O. (Universal Translation Machine) are Albert Einstein, Charles Darwin, Thomas Malthus Arnet, and Captain Tait, of the Tau Cetan Explorer Team.

Stan: Please tell our readers who you all are.

Einstein: They know the best for my theories of relativity. Do people still think that stuff is complicated?

Stan: Yeah. (*the next guess*) And you are...

Darwin: They know the best for my theory of the evolution of species.

Stan: And you are...

Goint: The Living Earth.

Stan: And you are Tait...

Tait: Tait. Yes. I'm on my seventh visit from Tau Ceti II. That's the second planet in orbit around the star Tau in what you call the constellation Cetus, The Whale.

Stan: Who constellation are we in?

Rosario Marquardt:
Portraits, Mirrors and Masks

When you hold a human body, one touches heaven.
Novalis

south beach
February 1993 Volume I No. III $ 2.75

south beach
May June 1993 Volume I No. V $ 3.00

PUBLISHER

SOUTH BEACH

MAGAZINE, INC.

ART DIRECTORS

JAMIE FERRAND

VICTORIA MADDOCKS

DESIGNERS

JAMIE FERRAND

VICTORIA MADDOCKS

PHOTOGRAPHERS

KENT BAKER

DAH-LEN

GALLEN MEI

ILLUSTRATORS

ROSARIO MARQUARDT

JONATHON ROSEN

contents
March April 1993 Volume I Number IV

Esquire

THE MAGAZINE FOR MEN

AUGUST 1992 · $2.50

Women We Love...

Candice Bergen
WOMAN OF THE YEAR

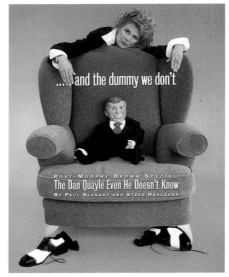

...and the dummy we don't

POST-MURPHY BROWN SPECIAL:
The Dan Quayle Even He Doesn't Know
BY PAUL SLANSKY AND STEVE RADLAUER

Esquire

THE MAGAZINE FOR MEN

FEBRUARY 1992 · $2.50

WHITE PEOPLE

THE TROUBLE WITH AMERICA

YOGA WITH
STING
AT THE RITZ

Can a rock star save the rain forest? The world? Himself?
By Doug Stanton

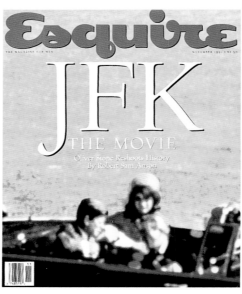

Esquire

THE MAGAZINE FOR MEN

NOVEMBER 1991 · $3.50

JFK
THE MOVIE

Oliver Stone Reshoots History
By Robert Sam Anson

PUBLISHER
HEARST CORPORATION
CREATIVE DIRECTOR
ROGER BLACK
ART DIRECTOR
RHONDA RUBENSTEIN
DESIGNERS
ROGER BLACK
AMID CAPECI
LEAH LOCOCO
RHONDA RUBENSTEIN
PHOTOGRAPHERS
DAVID BARRY
PEGGY SIROTA
ZAPRUDER FILM (STILL)

ESQUIRE

FOR A MAGAZINE with a design legacy as esteemed as *Esquire*'s any analysis is bound to evoke comparisons with the past. Over the past 50 years *Esquire* has visually evolved under various art directors, among them Henry Wolf (late '50s - '60s), Sam Antupit (mid '60s), Robert Priest (late '70s) and Roger Black (currently). The incarnation shown here produced in the early '90s by Roger Black and Rhonda Rubenstein attempts to graphically bring back *Esquire*'s wry wit, strong commentary, and elegant design. In the '60s *Esquire* was known for George Lois's posterlike, conceptual covers (few coverlines were attached to an image that was a virtual independent editorial statement). Today the marketplace demands that covers be more competitive, and so coverlines have become the bane of the magazine designer. In the *Esquire*'s shown here, they are mercifully kept to a minimum, and are more evocative than hardsell. Unprecedented in magazine design, the cover entitled "White People," almost entirely white, is both an intelligent, subtle, and courageous typeplay. Inside classic typography is used to frame strong (sometimes witty) original photography and illustration. But what truly defines *Esquire* are its surprising graphic features which comment on the comedy humane which provide space for artists and graphic commentators to express their points of view.

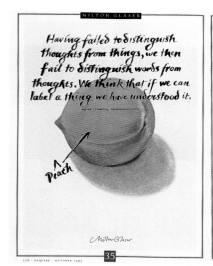

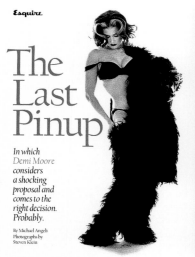

PUBLISHER
HEARST CORPORATION
CREATIVE DIRECTOR
ROGER BLACK
ART DIRECTOR
RHONDA RUBENSTEIN
DESIGNER
RHONDA RUBENSTEIN
PHOTOGRAPHER
STEVEN KLEIN
ILLUSTRATORS
MILTON GLASER
BARBARA KRUGER

21·C
DIGITAL NEWS
DISCOVER

SCIENCE & TECHNOLOGY

MONDO 2000
WIRED

knitting
patterns
FOR THE INSANE

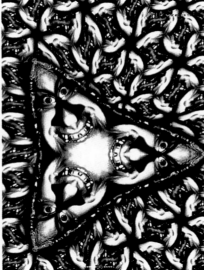

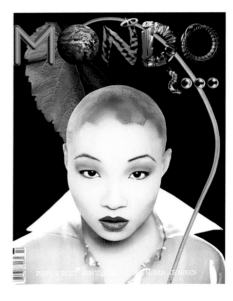

burnt
SUGAR
by David Kushner   photography by Todd V. Wolfson

PUBLISHER
FUN CITY MEGAMEDIA
ART DIRECTORS
HEIDE FOLEY
BART NAGEL
TOM PITTS
DESIGNERS
HEIDE FOLEY
BART NAGEL
TOM PITTS
PHOTOGRAPHERS
HEIDE FOLEY
TOM PITTS
J.K. POTTER
TODD WOLFSON
ILLUSTRATORS
HEIDE FOLEY
PANDER BROTHERS

CONTENTS

MONDO 2000

THE TITLE ALONE suggests a millennial experience awaits the reader of this magazine. *Mondo 2000* is the *Vogue*, *Time*, and *Life* of the late twentieth century. Its features are a mix of culture, technology, and fashion, and its design is appropriately eclectic, drawing on past, present, and future for inspiration. The unmistakable *Mondo 2000* logo is a colorful collage of futuristic/sci-fi icons that is potentially at odds with any cover image, but curiously it works in concert with most images. The logo is probably the most relatively consistent component of the overall design (although the *2000* changes each issue). Interior layouts do not follow a consistent theme but vary with the subjects. Like individual canvases, each spread is governed by an emotional rather than formal logic. Collage is a significant graphic device; photography — both tampered and untampered with — is the primary tool. Typographically, *Mondo 2000* runs the gamut of styles, from scripts to gothics, woodtype to digital fonts. While little real graphic experimentation is done, overall, *Mondo 2000*'s design, like its title suggests, appears to cover the visual world.

PUBLISHER
FUN CITY MEGAMEDIA
ART DIRECTORS
HEIDE FOLEY
BART NAGEL
TOM PITTS
DESIGNERS
HEIDE FOLEY
BART NAGEL
PHOTOGRAPHERS
HEIDE FOLEY
BART NAGEL
TOM PITTS
ILLUSTRATORS
KIECHI OTA
ERIC WHITE

GOLDEN WINDOW
ON A LOST WORLD

one ... in the late Eocene, a jaguar prowled through a fore bout thicket on the Caribbean island of Hispaniola. As the cat pushed by several seeds snagged onto its fur with their tiny hooks, a dispersal trick that often carried the seeds to fertile ground. This time, however, their tiny ride ended in a pool of resin, and immortality of a sort. Irritated by the seeds' spiky hooks, the cat rubbed against the trunk of a *Hymenaea* tree, a great resin producer of the American and African tropics. A wound in the tree's bark oozed a puddle of sticky stuff, and by chance the cat ...

TENS OF MILLIONS OF YEARS AGO THE RESIDENTS OF A CARIBBEAN FOREST WERE TRAPPED IN GLOWING
RIBBONS OF RESIN. TODAY THEY'RE TELLING SCIENTISTS WHAT THEIR WORLD WAS LIKE.   By Virginia Morell

PUBLISHER
WALT DISNEY
PUBLISHING
ART DIRECTOR
DAVID ARMARIO
DESIGNERS
DAVID ARMARIO
JAMES LAMBERTUS
PHOTOGRAPHERS
GEOF KERN
JEFFERY NEWBURY
STUART WATSON

USA

DISCOVER

HOW TO MAKE A SCIENCE and technology magazine accessible to the interested lay reader has been a challenge tackled by magazine designers for much of the twentieth century. From *Scientific American* which has traditionally taken a conservative, academic approach, to *Popular Science* which has adhered to a mass-market methodology, science has been the inspiration that has forced designers to scrap artifice in favor of clear visual communication. *Discover*, which is owned by The Disney Corporation, provides a good model: it is one of the more successfully art directed and designed general interest science magazines (including astronomy, medicine, physics, sex, nature, biology). Following traditional magazine format — a front, back and middle of the book with individual identities — it is nevertheless full of surprises as dictated by the material itself. *Discover*'s typography is contemporary without being trendy. Its graphic impact, however, is based on an expansive budget for large-scale projects that involve original photography, custom info-graphics (maps, diagrams, charts), and fine conceptual illustration by such practitioners as Ralph Steadman and Geof Kern. Some issues are general, but *Discover*'s most important contributions are its specials on global issues.

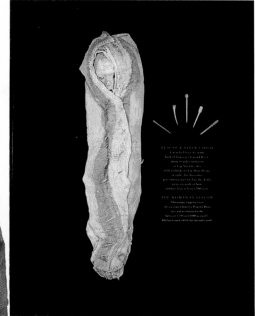

Amputees can feel missing hands grab a cup of coffee, missing feet itch, and missing legs ache.
Behind these ghostly sensations lies the secret of touch.

TOUCHING
THE
PHANTOM

BY JAMES SHREEVE

BLOOD MONEY

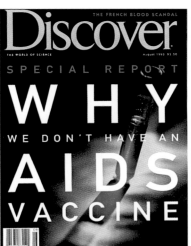

PUBLISHER
WALT DISNEY
PUBLISHING
ART DIRECTOR
DAVID ARMARIO
DESIGNERS
DAVID ARMARIO
JAMES LAMBERTUS
PHOTOGRAPHERS
GEOF KERN
JEFFERY NEWBURY
STUART WATSON
ILLUSTRATOR
RALPH STEADMAN

This is a
horror story,
and it's far from
over. It began in 1985 in
France, a country often envied for its
system of universal health care and tradition of medical
excellence. In one of the most shameful episodes of the
AIDS epidemic, physicians and government officials there
knowingly allowed at least a thousand people to receive
blood or blood products contaminated by the virus that
causes the disease. Three hundred of those people—
mainly hemophiliacs, many of them children—are
already dead. The rest are going to die, barring a miracle.

BY MARK HUNTER
ILLUSTRATIONS BY RALPH STEADMAN

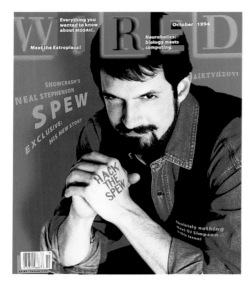

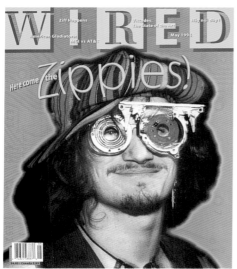

PUBLISHER
**WIRED VENTURES
LIMITED**
ART DIRECTORS
**BARBARA KUHR
JOHN PLUNKETT**
DESIGNERS
**ERIC ADIGARD
TRICIA McGILLIS
JOHN PLUNKETT**
PHOTOGRAPHERS
**KAREN MOSKOWITZ
FLORIS LEE OWENBERG
NEIL SELKIRK
BILL ZEMANEK**
ILLUSTRATOR
ERIC ADIGARD

WIRED

EVERY SO OFTEN a magazine comes along that is so wed to the zeitgeist that it becomes its mouthpiece — and if all the planets are aligned and the major distribution networks are clear — by virtue of its popularity, its design becomes the paradigm on which all others are based. *Wired* was the first mass-market magazine of the digital age — the *Rolling Stone* of the web-site-set — and its colorfully layered, hyper-text and raucous picture format has become the standard for how to design digitally in print. *Wired* is not, however, totally unique; it maintains conventional departments and a feature well; its typography is not as "revolutionary" as, say, *Emigre*. Neither is *Wired* experimental or cutting edge, but it is of the moment. In its amalgamation of classic and fashionable components, and in its effort to typographically interpret the digital gestalt, *Wired* is emblematic of an era, an ethos, and a generation. Critics may argue that *Wired* is too layered and, therefore, not reader friendly, but that presupposes that all magazines should follow a particular doctrine of legibility. *Wired* is subdued when it needs to be, wild when it has to be, and totally responsive to its twenty-first-century subject matter because that's the way it must be.

PUBLISHER
WIRED VENTURES LIMITED
ART DIRECTORS
BARBARA KUHR
JOHN PLUNKETT
DESIGNERS
ERIC ADIGARD
JOHN PLUNKETT
PHOTOGRAPHERS
DAVID McGLYNN
NEIL SELKIRK
ILLUSTRATOR
ERIC ADIGARD

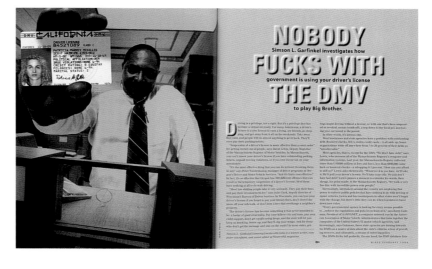

PUBLISHER
**THE AUSTRALIAN
COMMISSION FOR
THE FUTURE**
ART DIRECTOR
TERENCE HOGAN
DESIGNER
TERENCE HOGAN
EDITORS
**ASHLEY CRAWFORD
RAY EDGAR**
ILLUSTRATORS
**PETER CALLAS
IAN HAIG**

AUSTRALIA

21·C

WHEN USED AS a typeface 20 years ago, the rectilinear, computer-generated letterforms which are today found at the bottom of bank checks, suggested the future. Since computers have now overcome the constraints of such typographic cliches, what kind of design mannerism(s) now suggest the future? This was the challenge that faced *21·C* when it was founded by The Australian Commission for the Future, a government-backed organization that planned to address how technology, social sciences, and the arts would affect and be affected by the future. The answer was not to invent more futuristic alphabets or go into galaxies where no designer had gone before, but to take advantage of the current tools of design to make a forward looking (and thinking) magazine. With that, the conventions of magazines are more or less adhered to. The logo is an extrabold Futura *21·C* (for twenty-first century) that sits atop the usually chaotic cover illustration. The interior layouts are also characterized by an emphasis on controlled clutter — a varied assortment of blurbs, tiny pictures, sidebars, and other attention-grabbing material. Probably the most notable "futuristic" conceit is the many computer-generated color illustrations which give some of the pages the look of a computer screen.

21·C
A MAGAZINE OF CULTURE, TECHNOLOGY AND SCIENCE

chomsky
on the net

US$6.95
¥2200
Aus$9.95

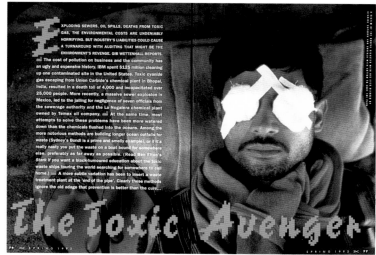

XPLODING SEWERS, OIL SPILLS, DEATHS FROM TOXIC GAS, THE ENVIRONMENTAL COSTS ARE UNDENIABLY HORRIFYING. BUT INDUSTRY'S LIABILITIES COULD CAUSE A TURNAROUND WITH AUDITING THAT MIGHT BE THE ENVIRONMENT'S REVENGE. GIB WETTENHALL REPORTS.

The cost of pollution on business and the community has an ugly and expensive history. IBM spent $125 million cleaning up one contaminated site in the United States. Toxic cyanide gas escaping from Union Carbide's chemical plant in Bhopal, India, resulted in a death toll of 4,000 and incapacitated over 25,000 people. More recently, a massive sewer explosion in Mexico, led to the jailing for negligence of seven officials from the sewerage authority and the La Negalera chemical plant owned by Temex oil company. At the same time, most attempts to solve these problems have been more watered down than the chemicals flushed into the oceans. Among the more notorious methods are building longer ocean outfalls for waste (Sydney's Bondi is a prime and smelly example), or if it's really nasty you put the waste on a boat bound for somewhere else, preferably as far away as possible. (Read Ben Elton's *Stark* if you want a black-humoured education about the toxic waste ships touring the world searching for somewhere to call home.) A more subtle variation has been to insert a waste treatment plant at the 'end of the pipe'. Clearly these methods ignore the old adage that prevention is better than the cure...

The Toxic Avenger

SPRING 1992 21·C 97

ONE MAN REVOLUTION

ROBERT JUNGK

Rick Slaughter talks to one of the founding fathers of futures studies, Robert Jungk, a major figure in the bid to confront the human and social implications of modern technology.

40 21·C WINTER 1992

I have to 'thank' Hitler in a certain sense, he threw me out of Germany and I had to go into the world. As a result of Hitler I became a planetary citizen.

PUBLISHER
THE AUSTRALIAN COMMISSION FOR THE FUTURE
ART DIRECTOR
TERENCE HOGAN
DESIGNERS
TERENCE HOGAN
CHRISTOPHER WALLER
EDITORS
ASHLEY CRAWFORD
RAY EDGAR
PHOTOGRAPHER
JOHN GOLLINGS
ILLUSTRATORS
PETER CROWTHER
CHRISTOPHER WALLER

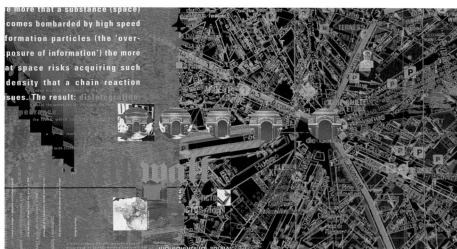

e more that a substance (space) comes bombarded by high speed formation particles (the 'over-posure of information') the more at space risks acquiring such density that a chain reaction sues. The result: disintegration

WINTER 1992 · ISSUE 8 · THE MAGAZINE OF THE AUSTRALIAN COMMISSION FOR THE FUTURE · $7.95

Totally Wired!
Tomorrow's Metropolis

21·C
PREVIEWS OF A CHANGING WORLD

The Future of Dreaming
Land Rights & Sacred Sites

THE GREAT DIVIDE
Leaders: What Future?   Youth: No Future?

ABC

BARRY JONES ON OUR AGEING SOCIETY · WOMEN IN SCIENCE
WILLIAM GIBSON · OLIVER SACKS · DAVID SUZUKI · RUPERT SHELDRAKE

PUBLISHER
**DIGITAL EQUIPMENT
OF CANADA**
ART DIRECTOR
MARK KOUDYS
DESIGNER
MARK KOUDYS
ILLUSTRATORS
BARRY BLITT
LOUIS FISHAUF
PHOTOGRAPHERS
ALAN ABRAMS
FRANCESCA LACAGNINA
RON BAXTER SMITH

The
Natural
habitat of

[innovative management]

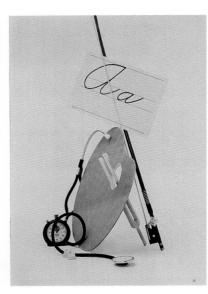

DIGITAL NEWS

DIGITAL NEWS

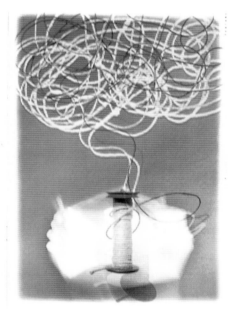

A view to the **entire** computing lifecycle

As though choosing the right hardware and software hasn't been decision enough. Yet now that seems like the good old days. All kinds of very good decisions, and perfectly workable point solutions, have led to a jigsaw puzzle of technological investment that takes specialized talent to manage. As companies, high-level generations to blend it into the envisioned big picture, multiple contracts to ensure its maintenance, and nothing short of genius to manage its enhancement. In such an environment, it's not

From site **planning** and start-up,

wonder that organizations are exploring ways to simplify or reduce their hands-on commitment to information technology management and get back to the business of running their business.

The desire to refocus on core businesses is leading organizations to consider a range of solutions from comprehensive outsourcing to consolidation of multivendor service contracts. Digital is responding to their needs. After all, information technology is Digital's core business and since Digital's own is the world's largest non-military network, the company is a seasoned implementer as well as a major vendor.

Digital is, then, constantly expanding and refining its customer services offerings to complement the changing business environments it supports. And it can do so from a uniquely strong position, by drawing on first-hand experience and evolving a long-time philosophy of supporting the entire computing lifecycle.

to disaster recovery and multivendor **maintenance**

To begin at the beginning: for many years, Digital has offered a number of services to aid customers at the earliest planning and design stages. For instance, specifically trained professional site specialists analyze how best an organization's overall system objectives can be satisfied by the appropriate computer facility design, and report in detail on the advantages and disadvantages of different design options. Total site designs, detailed drawings, specifications and cost estimates are developed next, based on an approval.

PUBLISHER
**DIGITAL EQUIPMENT
OF CANADA**
ART DIRECTOR
MARK KOUDYS
DESIGNER
MARK KOUDYS
ILLUSTRATOR
BARRY BLITT
PHOTOGRAPHERS
**ALAN ABRAMS
FRANCESCA LACAGNINA
RON BAXTER SMITH**

"The only way to stay competitive is to have the technology to make information available."

It's a perfect example of Canadian talent, ingenuity and savoir faire. Gandalf Technologies Inc., of Ottawa, is a leading designer and manufacturer of computer communications and networking products. Founded 20 years ago in Ottawa, the company holds 50 percent of the home market, with products development contributing to its small presence in the family growth into a data communications industry.

As first mention, for example, was also a first for the industry: a three-level monitor offering customers an efficient, low-cost alternative to more complex and extensive data transmission devices. Two years later, Gandalf earned another worldwide market with their ACX, the industry's first data switch. This innovation allowed users to communicate with computers from different switches, and with terminal and PC users in local and wide area environments. And the progress continues.

In 1991, Gandalf merged with Infotron between Corporation in New Jersey, thus strengthening its presence in the U.S. and the Pacific Rim and complementing its previous investments in Canada and the U.S. The merger allows Gandalf to combine its LAN expertise with Infotron's WAN to dual-rate its major enterprise-wide ownership.

Dave Binder,
Manager of Computer Operations,
Gandalf Technologies Inc.

DIGITAL NEWS

CANADA

SINCE IBM FIRST PUBLISHED its in-house magazine, *Think*, computer hardware companies have tried to produce magazines to tout their wares, stimulate investment, and otherwise put on a happy corporate face. That's what Digital, "the most advanced mainframe manufacturer in the world" did at great expense in producing a small in-house organ that went to several thousand users. When the company decided to produce a real magazine its designers began to consolidate resources to get the highest production and creative value for the money and produce a periodical that transcended the typical hardware "catalog." For one thing, the full-color, profusely illustrated *Digital News* did not show hardware images at all. In addition to its typographic distinction — starting with the unique "billboard" cover — an entire issue was illustrated by a single artist or photographer who addressed the magazine's themes conceptually, metaphorically, and allegorically. The designer says that this illustration approach also drove the design, "making each issue dramatically different, yet recognizable." Regrettably, this is one case where an intelligent design and editorial scheme did not save the magazine from the budget cuts of the early 1990s experienced throughout the computer industry.

CIVILIZATION
COLORS
CUT
DANCE INK
ENTERTAINMENT WEEKLY
GARBAGE
HARPER'S BAZAAR
LIFE
MÂP

CULTURE

MOJO
NICKELODEON
RAYGUN
ROLLING STONE
SAY
SPY
TENSION
VIBE
VISIONAIRE
W
WIGWAG

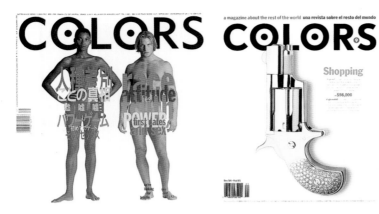

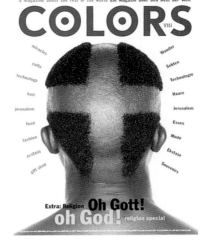

PUBLISHER
COLORS MAGAZINE SRL
ART DIRECTORS
MARK PORTER
PAUL RITTER
SCOTT STOWELL
DESIGNERS
GARY KOEPKE
PAUL RITTER
EDITOR
TIBOR KALMAN
PHOTOGRAPHERS
TODD EBERLE
OLIVIERO TOSCANI
ALBERT WATSON

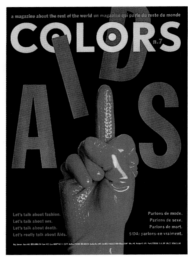

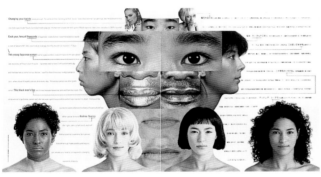

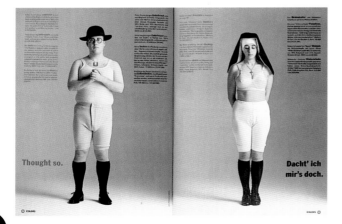

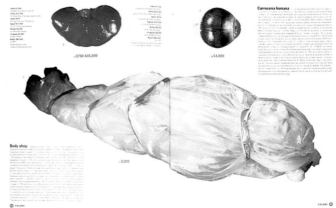

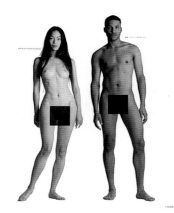

PUBLISHER
COLORS MAGAZINE SRL
ART DIRECTOR
SCOTT STOWELL
DESIGNERS
GARY KOEPKE
PAUL RITTER
EDITOR
TIBOR KALMAN
PHOTOGRAPHERS
TODD EBERLE
KATHY GROVE (RETOUCHING)
SERGIO MERLE
OLIVIERO TOSCANI
RONALD WOOLF/GLOBE

what if..?
こんなの、ありかな…?

games giochi

capelli come religione   hair is a religion

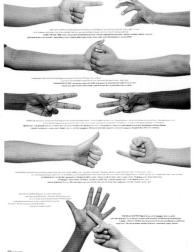

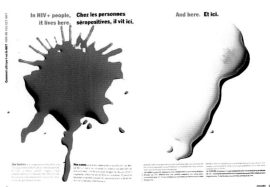

In HIV+ people, **Chez les personnes** it lives here. **séropositives, il vit ici.**   And here. **Et ici.**

COLORS

WITH ITS MISSION TO "create a new medium for the global language of young people who feel as closely connected to one another as to their individual cultures and countries," *Colors* is not unlike Atlas carrying the world upon its shoulders. The amazing thing is that after a dozen issues it doesn't seem to be suffering under the weight. *Colors* began as a total experiment — its size and shape changed with each thematic issue and its interior format was likewise unstable. After its first year, the size and format were reigned in, but its graphic approach and its editorial concerns — such as the dicey topics of race, AIDS, street life, and religion — continued to push a variety of limits — and buttons. *Colors* does not have clearly defined editorial departments, but it has special features that cover the thematic material using a variety of conceits, such as visually witty information graphics, full-page/extended caption "news" photographs, as well as more traditional articles. The graphic design is rooted in a sensationalistic use of gothic type (often printed in color) and non-rigid layouts that avoid stylistic hi jinx in favor of no-nonsense information. Printed on a comparatively cheap stock, the profuse full color is saturated and sometimes gaudy. But its the attention to detail — such as disturbing shifts in scale and startling juxtapositions — that give this magazine an allure and impact all its own.

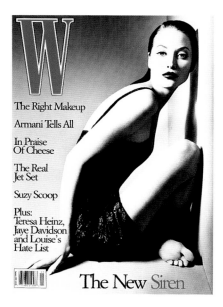

The New Siren

Nude Scene

USA

W

the Absolutes

A FASHION MAGAZINE can take part in the fashion experience by interpreting its subject with trendy type and layout conceits, or it can simply frame the material being featured with neutral, albeit elegant, graphic devices. *W* performs the latter function. As the weekly of the trade journal, *Women's Wear Daily*, *W* toes the line between industry news and retail display. Its covers set the tone for the mainstream approach to beauty and fashion inside. The tabloid format features a bold *W* logo in the left-hand corner, beneath it a bank of coverlines, and a strong, often silhouetted photograph of a model peering into the camera lens. Inside, simple, neutral typography sits against full-page photographs — nothing radical but perfectly in keeping with the surreal, often heroic mannerisms of fashion photography. Accessory shots are clean and clear, without the typographic clutter that often accompanies them. Scale is used to best advantage with a large detail of, for example, a pierced ear juxtaposed to a full body. What makes *W* so compelling is simplicity in a field where pyrotechnics are the norm.

W

Spring's
Look: Beyond
The Pale

Paris Couture

Are You
Too Thin?

Oscar Dressing

La Dolce Vita
In Argentina

Plus: Kate Capshaw,
Carolyne Roehm,
Vincent Perez, Linda
Evangelista & Suzy

PUBLISHER
FAIRCHILD
PUBLICATIONS
CREATIVE DIRECTOR
DENNIS FREEDMAN
DESIGN DIRECTORS
JEAN GRIFFIN
EDWARD LEIDA
ART DIRECTOR
KIRBY RODRIGUEZ
DESIGNERS
ROSALBA SIERRA
MYLA SORENSON
PHOTOGRAPHERS
MILES ALDRIDGE
RICHARD PIERCE
MICHAEL THOMPSON

NEGLECTED PARTS

TRESS TEST
Rich makeup almost nil, there's heightened focus on hair. Best hair looks need help to look great in winter. Try Kiehl's Herbal Hair Cream, Paul Mitchell's hair-sculpting Spray Gel, J.F. Lazartigue's Schoen Protein Hair Restorer and new for fall, Frenchlater Literature soft styling foam.

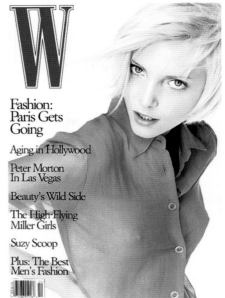

W

Fashion: Paris Gets Going

Aging in Hollywood

Peter Morton In Las Vegas

Beauty's Wild Side

The High-Flying Miller Girls

Suzy Scoop

Plus: The Best Men's Fashion

China Syndrome
Rich embroideries, bright satins, frogs and high collars speak of the mysterious East.

PHOTOGRAPHED BY SATOSHI SAIKUSA

midnight cowgirl

PUBLISHER
FAIRCHILD
PUBLICATIONS
CREATIVE DIRECTOR
DENNIS FREEDMAN
DESIGN DIRECTORS
JEAN GRIFFIN
EDWARD LEIDA
ART DIRECTOR
KIRBY RODRIGUEZ
DESIGNERS
ROSALBA SIERRA
MYLA SORENSON
PHOTOGRAPHERS
MICHAEL THOMPSON
RAYMOND MEIER
CRAIG McDEAN
SATOSHI SAIKUSA

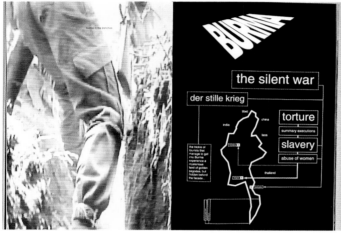

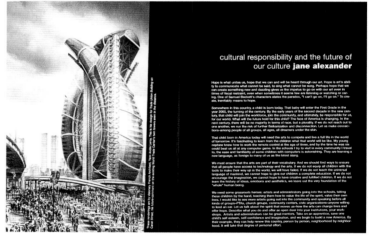

PUBLISHER
MAP PUBLICATIONS, INC.
ART DIRECTOR
**ROBERT BERGMAN-
UNGAR**
DESIGNER
**ROBERT BERGMAN-
UNGAR**
ARTISTS
PETER ASTROM
MARK JOSEPH
TRICIA KRAUSS
VANN LEROI
DONALD LESKO
OSAMU SATO
PHOTOGRAPHERS
**ROBERT BERGMAN-
UNGAR**
JEAN BAPTISTE MONDINO
DAVID SEIDNER

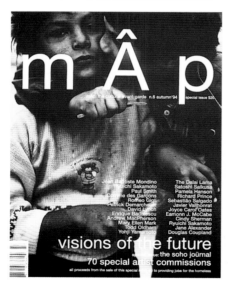

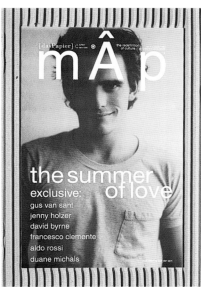

enrique badulescu
(Mexico)

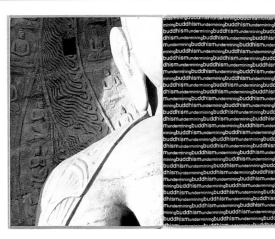

PUBLISHER
MAP PUBLICATIONS, INC.
ART DIRECTOR
ROBERT BERGMAN-UNGAR
DESIGNER
ROBERT BERGMAN-UNGAR
ARTIST
ENRIQUE BADULESCU
PHOTOGRAPHERS
DANIEL SCHWARTZ
DAVID SEIDNER
GUS VAN SANT

MÂP
USA

"*MÂP* WAS CREATED specifically to have no design challenges or obstacles, to be completely free of constraint," says its editor. In fact the real challenge for this high-quality quarterly "with a truly unique view of avant-garde culture" is how one issue will be totally different from the next. Each quarter *MÂP* is devoted to a different theme, such as "Visions of the Future" and "The Summer of Love," and draws upon collaborators from all creative fields all over the globe. It counts among its contributors David Lynch, The Dalai Lama, David Byrne and Joyce Carol Oates. *MÂP*'s texts and visuals are enhanced by a design strategy that evolves from the material itself. Writers, editors and designers team up to produce a package that fits the overall social and cultural concerns of the magazine. *MÂP* is therefore a hybrid. It does not follow traditional journal or magazine conventions, save for having a cover and back cover. Its beginning, middle, and end are a confluence of visual and typographic "experiences," portfolios, and posterlike spreads. Its perfect-bound, square-back format suggests a lavish picture book rather than a magazine, but it is intended to be sold on newsstands on a periodic basis. *MÂP*'s covers are generally geared to provoke and pique interest, as the current crop of fashion advertising suggests an aura, rather than a strong idea. But once inside, *MÂP* delivers ideas, impressions, and commentary galore.

FALL 1994 VOLUME 5, NUMBER 3

SWAN SONG FOR NUREYEV
PATTI SMITH, 3

TAMARA TOUMANOVA
WENDY LESSER, 4

RALPH LEMON
CRAIG BROMBERG, 6

JULIO GONZALEZ
NANCY REYNOLDS, 10

KATHY ROSE
DON McDONAGH, 12

LA RONDE
NANCY DALVA, 14

BODY LANGUAGE
RICHARD B. WOODWARD, 18

SILENT MOVES
MARGO JEFFERSON, 22

ON THE TRACKS
TOBI TOBIAS, 28

KEYED UP
TORENE SVITIL, 34

EILEEN THOMAS
JOSEF ASTOR, 36

THE RULES OF THE GAME
TOBI TOBIAS, 38

PUBLISHER
DANCE INK, INC.
ART DIRECTOR
J. ABBOTT MILLER
DESIGNER
J. ABBOTT MILLER
PHOTOGRAPHERS
JOSEF ASTOR
ANDREW ECCLES
MARSHA LIPPMAN
HELMUT NEWTON

122

USA
DANCE INK

DANCE INK, a uniquely literate, small circulation, quarterly journal devoted to a visual performance art is a case study of magazine design evolution. As a whole *Dance Ink* is a testament to the proposition that a traditional typographic approach with contemporaneous applications is more viable, and curiously more mutable, than those trendy, anti-design approaches that rapidly grow old and tiresome. The development of *Dance Ink*'s distinctive character seems to have been intelligently planned and measured over the past two years. The first couple of issues were resolutely spare owing to limited means. The decision to print on uncoated stock using no more than two colors further underscored its shoestring budget. Early *Dance Ink*s were visually noteworthy for striking black and white or duotone covers of dancers in heroic, contorted, and even comic poses situated under or over a logo that changed from issue to issue. The cover was simple, though bold and the interior design was more sedate with columns of ragged type simply laid out on a grid without any overlapping, layering or inter-line disbursement of supplementary text in the current typographic fashion that tries to suggest various voices or echo video screens. By the Summer 1993 issue, full color was introduced on the cover, with some spot color on selected inside pages. The paperstock, though still comparatively cheap, was also upgraded to give the magazine a tactile sensation. In fact, *Dance Ink* seems more like an arts catalog than a commercial magazine.

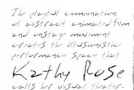

DANCE INK

SUMMER 1994

PUBLISHER
DANCE INK, INC.
ART DIRECTOR
J. ABBOTT MILLER
DESIGNER
J. ABBOTT MILLER
PHOTOGRAPHERS
ANDREW ECCLES
GEORGE PLATT LYNES
HERB RITTS
JOANNE SAVIO

DANCEDANCE
DANCEDANCEDANCE
DANCE   DANCE
DANCE   DANCE
DANCE   DANCE
DANCE   DANCE
DANCE   DANCE
DANCE DANCE
DANCE DANCE
DANCEDANCEDANCE
DANCEDANCEDANCE

INK

WINTER 1994/95 $5

tamara toumanova

portrait
of a
ballerina

WENDY LESSER

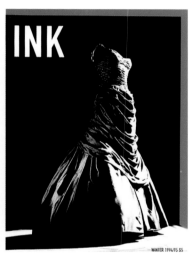

ralph

dance

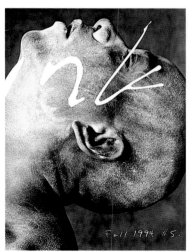

ink

Fall 1994 #5.

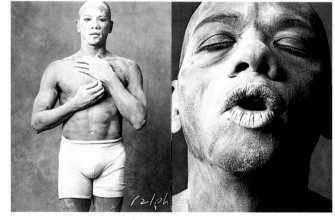

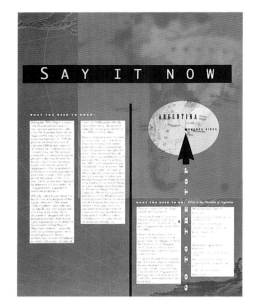

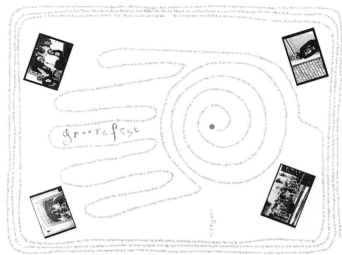

PUBLISHER
SAY MAGAZINE
ART DIRECTORS
ALICIA JOHNSON
HAL WOLVERTON
DESIGNERS
KAT SAITO
HAL WOLVERTON
ILLUSTRATOR
KAT SAITO

Unequal Justice

ANARCHY
STARVATION CLAIMS
Somalia

124

PUBLISHER
SAY MAGAZINE
ART DIRECTORS
ALICIA JOHNSON
HAL WOLVERTON
DESIGNERS
KAT SAITO
HAL WOLVERTON
PHOTOGRAPHERS
VARIOUS
ILLUSTRATOR
KAT SAITO

SAY

POLITICAL AND SOCIAL messages can be conveyed with and without strong graphic impact. Some propagandists argue that design should play a neutral role allowing the content to speak for itself, others counter that to attract attention in an image-saturated world the graphics must equal if not surpass the text. Such is the challenge for *Say*, Amnesty International's bimonthly student/youth membership publication. It must at once convey harsh realities of the geo-political world and appeal to young potential supporters who have been weaned on MTV. "We chose to eliminate gruesome imagery whenever alternate images were available," say the designers. "The information, combined with the emotional, and as often as possible, hopeful images allows a reader to experience simultaneously the beauty of the human spirit and the potential for human ugliness." Consequently, *Say* makes its message clear through an aesthetic style consistent with contemporary typographic methodologies. Type is layered and smashed, but never illegible or inaccessible. Typography is a panacea for a tight budget for art and photographs, which are routinely donated. Budgetary concerns also led to the use of two colors, no black, providing a broader range of options in the production of each issue. *Say* is alone in the field of "human rights magazines for young audiences" and therefore sets a standard for how this critical information is communicated.

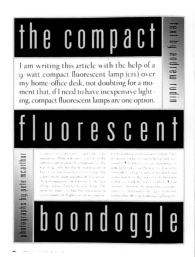

GARBAGE

WHEN IT BEGAN in the late 1980s *Garbage* was, shall we say, garbage from a design point of view. In recent years, however, the magazine had become a paradigm of fine design in the service of some rather difficult subject matter. It is therefore a shame that as of 1995 it is no longer published. *Garbage* contained conventional magazine features — a front, back, and middle of the book — but they were designed to pique the senses and enhance reading pleasure. Of course garbage is not the most inviting subject, but in an age when waste management is of primary environmental interest in many people's minds, this magazine offered a curious balance of cautionary, self-help, and participatory articles. That its elegant typography, smart conceptual illustration, and witty cover and interior design made the product "smell" that much sweeter, was a tribute to a designer that knew how to package the goods for maximum impact. The front-of-the-book news shorts and factoids, which are often the most staid part of a magazine, were designed consistently with flair, allowing for large and small stories to share the same space. Although this was a relatively consistent format, its original design offered enough variations to keep the section from becoming stale. The features, on the other hand, were always designed differently, often responding to the subject matter, with expansive intro type treatments and generous use of original illustration. *Garbage* was not only smart for specialized magazines, but was a model for all contemporary magazines.

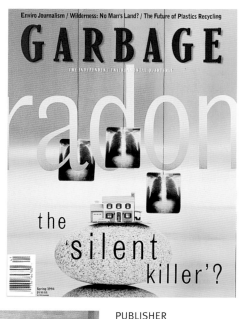

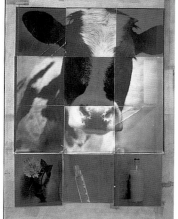

PUBLISHER
DOVETALE PUBLISHERS
ART DIRECTOR
PATRICK MITCHELL
DESIGNER
PATRICK MITCHELL
PHOTOGRAPHERS
THE DOUGLAS BROTHERS
ABRAMS LACAGNINA
PETE McARTHUR
ILLUSTRATOR
AMY GUIP

· trees ·

the South of rainforests, the habitat of spotted owls, children on arbor day ... the science behind the symbolism, and why it matters

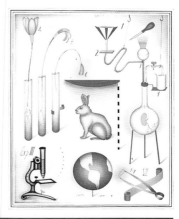

Why We Need Animal Testing

Animal research is vital for assessing the impacts of contaminants on the environment and human health. Pioneering efforts are underway to develop alternatives to animal testing. But animals are still needed for validating most test results. Though imperfect, a mouse remains the best model for man. So what are the consequences if activists impede essential animal research?

BY BILL BREEN

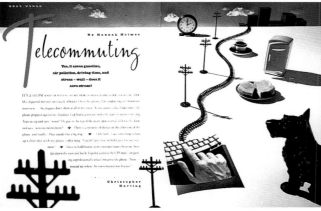

By Hannah Holmes

Telecommuting

Yes, it saves gasoline, air pollution, driving time, and stress – wait – does it save stress?

Christopher Harting

Reuse It!

Among the 3R's, Reuse is an overlooked stepchild compared to its celebrated kin, Reduce and Recycle. Introducing innovators who have pioneered creative, even profitable ways to Reuse our well used possessions.

by Hannah Holmes

what the hell are we fighting for

crying "backlash," an embattled movement struggles to articulate a vision of sustainable environmentalism for the future. by robert braile

using the internet · toxic cleanup with microbes · chemical agriculture

GARBAGE

THE INDEPENDENT ENVIRONMENTAL QUARTERLY · FALL 1994

the environmental movement, from edward abbey's stirring iconoclasm to the moans of "backlash" ...

what next?

PUBLISHER
DOVETALE PUBLISHERS
ART DIRECTOR
PATRICK MITCHELL
DESIGNER
PATRICK MITCHELL
PHOTOGRAPHERS
FREDERIK BRODEN
CHRISTOPHER HARTING
ILLUSTRATORS
KATHY BOAKE
SETH JABEN
GORDON STUDER
GARY TANHAUSER
NICHOLAS VITACCO

VISIONAIRE

HISTORY REVEALS THAT there have been many attempts at creating the magazine as an artifact. *Visionaire* follows a tradition that includes *Fluxus*, *Aspen*, *SMS*, and other mags in a box, but applies its own standards. This quarterly "limited edition" (1,000 of the first issue were printed) with a hefty cover price to offset the elimination of advertising, is intended to give freedom to contributing artists. *Visionarie* "treats the magazine concept as a unique, precious, collectible thing, as opposed to being disposable," says its editor. Hence a considerable amount of time-consuming handwork is done to achieve this distinction, including pop-ups in No. 6. Assembled like an artist's portfolio, Visionarie's form and content are indeed one. The individual contents include prints, photographs, and exhibition catalogs, each "designed" with its own integrity and personality. The contents are packaged in a box with a constantly changing veneer which alternates between wild visuals and understated typography. Although this magazine is avidly concerned with design, it is not self consciously designed in the way that most magazines are defined by visual pacing. Visionaire, however, is the sum of its movable and removable parts; it is literally a magazine in flux.

PUBLISHER
**VISIONAIRE
PUBLISHING CO.**
ART DIRECTOR
STEPHEN GAN

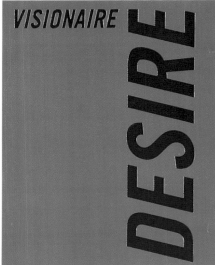

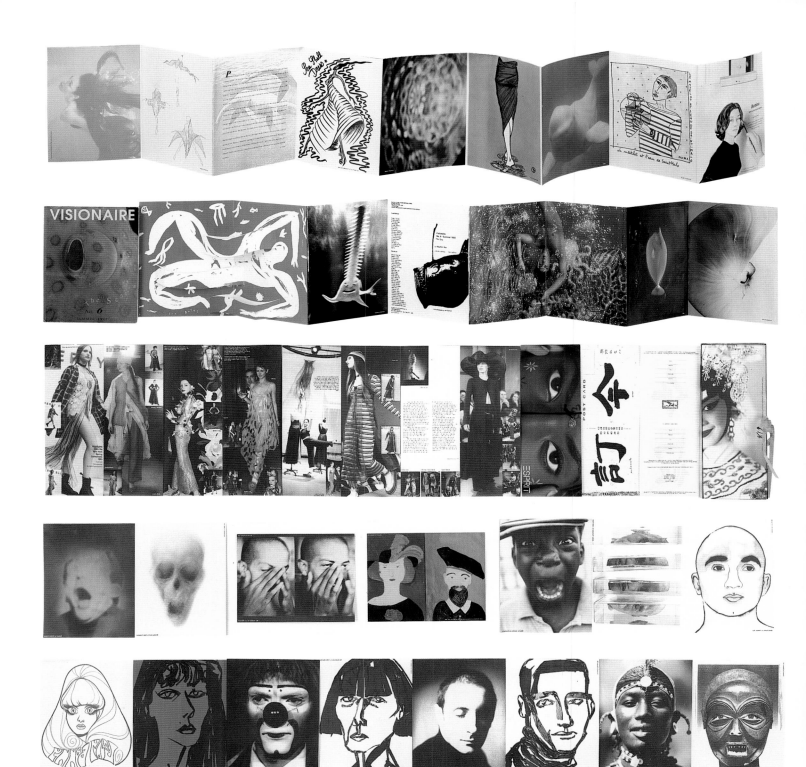

PUBLISHER
**VISIONAIRE
PUBLISHING CO.**
ART DIRECTOR
STEPHEN GAN

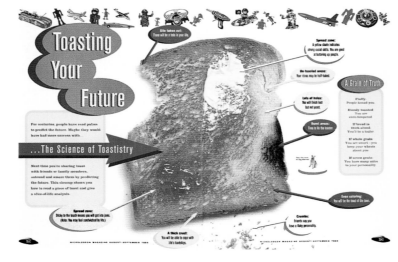

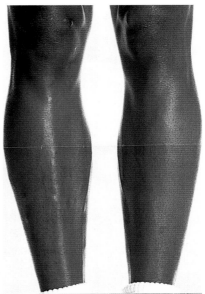

PUBLISHER
NICKELODEON
DESIGN DIRECTOR
ALEXANDER ISLEY
ART DIRECTOR
NOEL CLARO
ASSOCIATE ART
DIRECTOR
ALEXA MULVIHILL
DESIGNER
PETER GATTO
PHOTOGRAPHERS
GREG MILLER
BONNIE SHIFFMAN/
PARAMOUNT PICTURES

Cont.

Stimulocity
stim-u-LAH-si-tee:
Where music best plays work and and

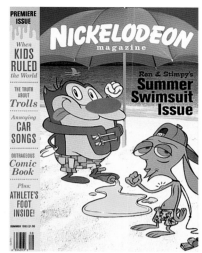

PUBLISHER
NICKELODEON
DESIGN DIRECTOR
ALEXANDER ISLEY
ART DIRECTOR
NOEL CLARO
ASSOCIATE ART
DIRECTOR
ALEXA MULVIHILL
DESIGNERS
DAVID ALBERTSON
PETER GATTO
ILLUSTRATORS
DAVID ALBERTSON
DAVID SHELDON

NICKELODEON

USA

MAGAZINES DESIGNED for kids are naturally carnivals in print. A variety of typefaces, comic and cartoon illustrations, numerous boxes, blurbs, and sidebars are all elements of most kid publications. *Nickelodeon Magazine* is no different, but it is unique. Based on the raucous graphic identity of the Nickelodeon television network, this magazine contains on-air ideas inserted in two-dimensional space, and gives the young readers a potpourri of visual experiences for immediate and long term gratification. And yet, while presenting a chaotic appearance, *Nickelodeon* is carefully structured for optimum editorial flow. Beginning with a crazy table of contents, the magazine moves from regular designed columns into uniquely composed features, to comics and funny pages, and finally to the back of the book — with various inserts and pullouts in between. There is never a dull moment, nor is there a totally undisciplined page. It takes great skill and talent to make something appear like lunacy incarnate but actually be tightly controlled. The cover is basically the same each issue. The Nickelodeon logo is identifiable to children and adults alike, and the teasers down the left side of the image offer new ingredients in the same package. A kid will never get lost inside, either. While each story is uniquely designed, nothing is illogical.

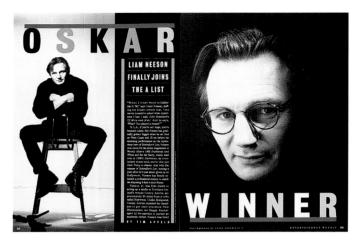

PUBLISHER

**ENTERTAINMENT
WEEKLY INC.**

DESIGN DIRECTORS

MICHAEL GROSSMAN

ROBERT NEWMAN

ART DIRECTORS

JILL ARMUS

ELIZABETH BETTS

MARK MICHAELSON

DESIGNERS

JILL ARMUS

JULIE SCHRADER

PHOTOGRAPHERS

LOOMIS DEAN/CAMERA

PRESS GLOBAL PHOTOS

JOHN GOODMAN

FABRIZIO LIPARI

STEVEN MEISEL

FRANK OCKENFELS 3

**TOR RICHARDSON/
SCAN FOTO**

JEFFREY THURNHER

DIEGO UCHITEL

RAUL VEGA

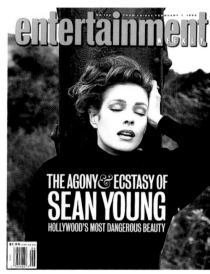

ENTERTAINMENT WEEKLY

SINCE ENTERTAINMENT is America's biggest (indeed most exportable) industry, why shouldn't it have the best entertainment magazine in the world? *Entertainment Weekly* certainly fits that editorial bill, but it also rates high on the design charts as well. Following its own editorial logic, *Entertainment Weekly* is organized into sections — Film, TV, Music, etc. — each graphically identified, not by some cute icon, but rather a color-coded tab. Within each section the typographic hierarchy is similar throughout the magazine — a lead story, followed by shorter reviews, sidebars and info-graphics. The cover, which tends to lean towards large pictures with excessive, though nevertheless tastefully designed, gothic coverlines introduces the lead story, which is routinely designed differently from the rest of the magazine. The feature typography, influenced no doubt by *Rolling Stone*'s eclecticism, is smartly handled to frame the usually original photography of personalities. Illustration is also used to smart advantage with a score of fine caricaturists called in to pay homage and/or lampoon the various celebrities. Despite its consistent format and the fact that avid readers and entertainment fans might anticipate the lead story, *Entertainment Weekly* is always a surprise. Much has to do with the balance between news, profiles, and reviews and the way that these elements are always designed to give the readers a sense of familiarity, while at the same time tweaking their senses with unique visuals.

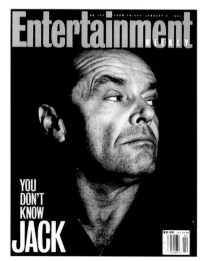

PUBLISHER
ENTERTAINMENT WEEKLY INC.
DESIGN DIRECTORS
MICHAEL GROSSMAN
ROBERT NEWMAN
ART DIRECTORS
JILL ARMUS
MARK MICHAELSON
DESIGNER
MIRIAM CAMPIZ
PHOTOGRAPHERS
PEGGY SIROTA
ALASTAIR THAIN
ILLUSTRATOR
CALEF BROWN

MOJO

PUBLISHER
EMAP METRO
ART DIRECTOR
ANDY COWLES
DESIGNERS
ANDY COWLES
STEPHEN FAWCETT
PHOTOGRAPHERS
SYLVIA PITCHER
MARK SELIGER/OUTLINE
CHRIS WALTER/
PHOTOFEATURES

SO MANY MAGAZINES currently cover the rock and roll scene(s) that the challenge for any designer is to create a truly unique graphic personality. *Mojo* attempts to carve out a persona through striking original photography and expressionistic typography. One of the most amazing photographs *Mojo* has published is a simple portrait of Cream drummer Ginger Baker, his once sculpted features now craggy with age and hard from experience. Other equally striking photos included old blues greats rarely, if ever, found in other rock publications. In addition to including the leading movers and shakers, *Mojo* does an admirable job of covering many of the personalities and phenomena ignored by other magazines. Maintaining a middle road course between *Rolling Stone* and *RayGun*, *Mojo*'s graphic design, though not as innovative as the others, beautifully frames the material. Its covers are decidedly commercial, with an excessive number of coverlines handled with as much taste as such typographic protuberances allow. Inside, though, the classically based typography frames the photography and conceptual illustration, and does not overpower the editorial content. Bucking the tendency for contemporary rock magazines to exude hipness through chaotic design, *Mojo* designs its varied components so that they work together harmoniously.

PHOTOGRAPH BY
JACK ENGLISH

"Do Toad!"

No, on second thoughts, don't. "I'm an actor, not a drummer," Ginger Baker tells Tom Hibbert.

SLY STONE The riotous life of funk's doomed superstar

MOJO
The Rock'n'Roll Magazine

AUGUST 1994 £2.25

Fairports
Spin Doctors
New Stones CD
Eagles live

The Clash
FROM WESTWAY TO BROADWAY

UNBELIEVABLE!
OJ Simpson
& Tim Buckley's
lost movie

FABLES OF THE FOUR-HEADED
MONSTER

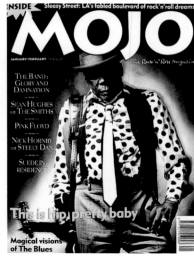

There's the conventional approach to writing, recording, the universe and everything else. And then there's the perverse total opposite, the R.E.M. method. MOJO talks to the producers, managers and musicians who've been on the inside and seen how it works. By Dave DiMartino, Jim Irvin and Mark Ellen. Photographs by Nigel Parry.

INSIDE Sleazy Street: LA's fabled boulevard of rock'n'roll dreams

MOJO
The Rock'n'Roll Magazine

JANUARY/FEBRUARY 1994

THE BAND:
GLORY AND
DAMNATION

SEAN HUGHES
on THE SMITHS

PINK FLOYD

NICK HORNBY
on STEELY DAN

SUEDE IN
RESIDENCE

This is hip, pretty baby

Magical visions
of The Blues

PUBLISHER
EMAP METRO
ART DIRECTOR
ANDY COWLES
DESIGNERS
ANDY COWLES
STEPHEN FAWCETT
PHOTOGRAPHERS
JACK ENGLISH
RAY FURY (RETOUCHING)
NIGEL PARRY/KATZ
MARK SELIGER/OUTLINE
PAUL SLATTERY/RETNA
VAL WILMER
ILLUSTRATOR
JANET WOOLLEY/ARENA

Father, Son
& Hillbilly Cat

※ Boy-King/Fertility God brings wonder and prosperity to the land, is cut down but manages to transcend death. . . The ballooning Cult Of Elvis is turning into a fully-fledged religion. ※

By Mick Farren

"Come on, Bill, let's take them for an old country rock. Let's go back down the Rappahanock, down Tappahanock way. Look at Bill while everybody rocks. Get that old rock, Bill. Everybody rock. Old folks rock. Young folks rock. Boys rock. Girls rock. Trot back, man, and let me rock. Rock me, sis, rock me. Rock me till I sweat. Trot back, folks, let your pappy rock. Pappy knows how. Children rock. Sister Ernestine, show your pappy how you rock. Mighty fine, boys, rock it, rock it till the cows come home. Whip that box, Bill, whip it. Too sad, I mean too sad for the public. Now up the country, back down the country again on that old rock. Rappahanock, Tappahanock. Cross the river, boys, cross the river. Man, it's sporty. Play it, Bill, play it till the sergeant comes."

Models looked different about a year ago. They seemed smaller, tired, almost timid. And all because they weren't wearing mascara.

But now it's a thrill to see Claudia Schiffer glammed out and Nadja Auermann cosmetically larger-than-life. Even Kate Moss seems to have added stature. Lashings of black are now officially resanctioned, and we should all rejoice.

For the extreme velvety eye, makeup artist Marie-Jose Lafontaine recommends brushing on up to three coats from root to tip, emphasizing the roots. For balance, lower lashes also need a neat coat or two, she adds. Clumps can be gently combed out with a lash brush. (Lancôme's new Intencils mascara, designed not to clump, is applied with a "peanut" brush, which is wider at the ends in order to thicken and lengthen lashes at the corners.)

Makeup artist Fulvia Farolfi likes Clinique Naturally Glossy Mascara, which she applies close to the roots—moving the brush back and forth horizontally before applying to the rest of the lash. ("It is not pretty to see a light root," she explains.) For the bottom lash, she cleans the brush and applies just color, not visible mascara. That's nice, but as Lafontaine asks, why not "pile it on"? —*Gale Hanson*

The Black Forest

Extreme mascara is back. Choose your favorite brush, but always wear black.

anatomy of a suit

The Purity Principle

PUBLISHER

THE HEARST

CORPORATION

CREATIVE DIRECTOR

FABIEN BARON

ART DIRECTORS

JOEL BERG

JOHAN SVENSSON

DESIGNERS

PAUL EUSTARE

JOHAN SVENSSON

PHOTOGRAPHERS

TIM BURTON

RAYMOND MEIER

DAVID SIMS

MARIO SORRENTI

True Knit

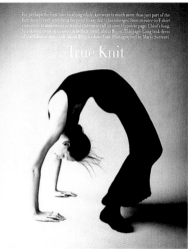

HARPER'S BAZAAR

Cool
Classics
for Winter

Split-Second Chic:
the working wardrobe

The Seductive Tux

Sandals on Ice

Domestic Violence:
Wealth and Power
Can't Protect You

Nadja Auermann's Short Cut

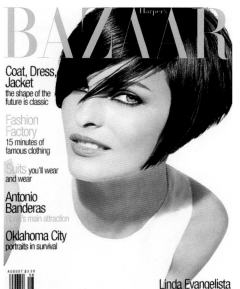

Coat, Dress,
Jacket
the shape of the
future is classic

Fashion
Factory
15 minutes of
famous clothing

Suits you'll wear
and wear

Antonio
Banderas
Spain's main attraction

Oklahoma City
portraits in survival

Linda Evangelista

THIS IS A MAGAZINE with a design tradition like no other in this book. From its early covers, designed by art deco *graphiste*, Erte, to its modern format design by Alexey Brodovitch and later by art directors Henry Wolf, Marvin Isreal, Bea Feitler and Ruth Ansel, *Harper's Bazaar* has been the vessel of fine design, photography, and conceptual illustration. More than a mere magazine about fashion, it has been a fashion-setting magazine. When Fabien Barron took the reigns he reintroduced some of the elegance that had been lost from the early Brodovitch (and his acolytes') designs. Bringing back Bodoni was like restoring jewels to a crown. But Barron was not content just to reprise the tried and true, he added his own distinctive typographic touch — the overlapping of letters in what first appears chaotic, but ultimately comes into focus as perfectly readable. Combining his personal type vocabulary with strong photography; his rejection of the new-wave ornament in favor of generous white space; and a return to simple conceptual approaches rather than ostentatious pyrotechnics has brought *Harper's Bazaar* back into visual prominence as it enhances its editorial viewpoint. Although the magazine has stayed a rather steady course after the initial surge of energy — not veering too far into uncharted waters — it is still one of the finest magazines in its genre today.

Pure
Simplicity

PUBLISHER
**THE HEARST
CORPORATION**
CREATIVE DIRECTOR
FABIEN BARON
ART DIRECTORS
**JOEL BERG
JOHAN SVENSSON**
DESIGNER
JOHAN SVENSSON
PHOTOGRAPHERS
**PATRICK DEMARCHELIER
PETER LINDBERGH**

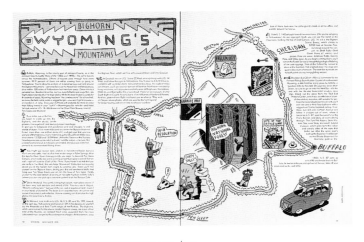

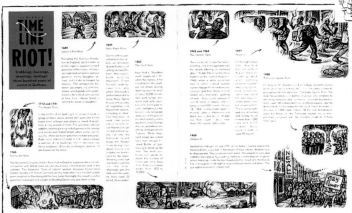

PUBLISHER

**THE WIGWAG MAGAZINE
COMPANY**

ART DIRECTOR

PAUL DAVIS

DESIGNERS

**JEANINE ESPOSITO
ALEXANDRA GINNS
RISA ZAITSCHEK**

ILLUSTRATORS

**JULIAN ALLEN
IVAN CHERMAYEFF
PAUL DAVIS
MAIRA KALMAN
MARK ROSENTHAL
BILL RUSSELL**

PUBLISHER
**THE WIGWAG MAGAZINE
COMPANY**
ART DIRECTOR
PAUL DAVIS
DESIGNERS
**ALEXANDRA GINNS
RISA ZAITSCHEK**
ILLUSTRATORS
**ANN BAYER
JEFFREY FISHER
JOSH GOSFIELD
JOSÉ ORTEGA**

USA

WIGWAG

WIGWAG FOLDED before it had a chance to develop out of its adolesence, but not before it had made an impact on magazine design. Founded as a livelier, but no less literate, alternative to the *New Yorker*, *WigWag* attempted to wed classic design principles to new-wave methods. The title itself suggests vitality — and wit — which is eschewed in most mainstream magazines. Its covers were celebrations of fine conceptual illustration; both veteran and neophyte illustrators were given an empty canvas on which to create independent artworks that contributed to the magazine's overall personality. To avoid the necessity for coverlines that would obscure the art, a swirly, diecut flap announced the magazine's contents. Inside *WigWag* was a carnival of imagery. Illustrated column heads were recast for each issue by painters, collagists, and sculptors. Feature illustrations were given generous space, and often details or additional pieces were carried throughout the layouts. The typography was based on a traditional foundation, but was routinely skewed to add elements of surprise. In addition, *WigWag* introduced odd features, such as bedtime stories, family trees of cars and comic book heroes, which gave it an air of unpredictability.

Susan Moritz takes a gardener's look at what florists do to flowers.

Sven Birkerts exposes the Vile Body.

PUBLISHER
TIME INC. MAGAZINES
DIRECTOR OF DESIGN
TOM BENTKOWSKI
DESIGNERS
TOM BENTKOWSKI
NORA SHEEHAN
PHOTOGRAPHERS
EDDIE ADAMS
DAVID BURNETT
ROBERT MAPPLETHORPE
LENNART NILSSON
BILL RAY
RAY RIPPER
PAUL SCHUTZER
EDWARD STEICHEN

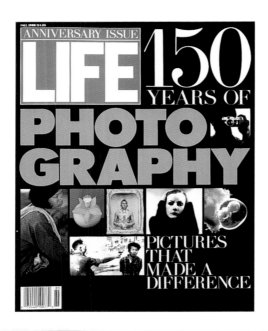

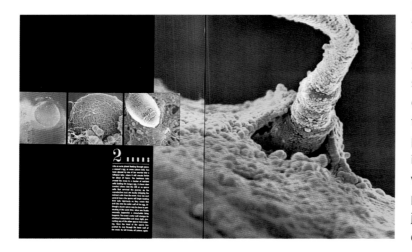

LIFE

IF ANY MAGAZINE HAS had an extraordinary effect on the way people view their world, *Life* is that magazine. Generations were weaned on *Life*'s groundbreaking photojournalism. And before television, *Life* was an eye on — at times a microscopic view of — the world. America's most profound visual icons were revealed on its pages, and the world's most poignant images were conveyed to millions. Originally, *Life*'s graphic design merely framed the photos; typographic play was confined to a few functional typefaces — the pictures were the stars. In the 1970s *Life*'s impact diminished as electronic media gave the public more immediate visual satisfaction. It folded briefly only to be revived as a monthly, still emphasizing photojournalism but with a more profound design presence. In the 1990s the magazine was reduced in size. Although it continues to publish strong photographic essays, its graphic design has become more than a neutral frame; it is the glue that binds many disparate stories together. While still governed by its photographic content, typography and layout strengthen the presentation and provide entry points for the reader to engage in the magazine. Changes in the way the public "reads", indeed appreciates, imagery has made it necessary to provide as much graphic accessibility as possible. In this sense, *Life* continues its journalistic tradition but allows design to carry much of the weight.

PUBLISHER
TIME INC. MAGAZINES
DIRECTOR OF DESIGN
TOM BENTKOWSKI
DESIGNERS
TOM BENTKOWSKI
MARTI GOLON
MIMI PARK
NORA SHEEHAN
PHOTOGRAPHERS
RICHARD AVEDON
ALBERT FACELLY
JACQUES LANGEVIN
JACQUES-HENRI LARTIGUE
DAVID LITTSCHWAGER
SUSAN MIDDLETON
LENNART NILSSON
MARIALBA RUSSO
MARINA YURCHENKO

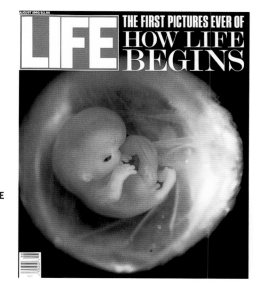

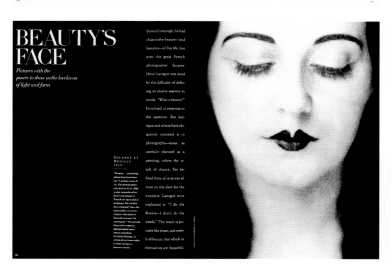

PUBLISHER
ROCKIN' ON, INC.
ART DIRECTOR
HIDEKI NAKAJIMA
DESIGNER
HIDEKI NAKAJIMA
PHOTOGRAPHERS
YORAM KAHANA
STEVEN KLEIN
ELLIOT LANDY
STEVEN MEISEL
ALBERT WATSON

KEANU REEVES
Bouddha, c'est lui!
Dans le film de Bertolucci, il confirm
qu'il est l'un des acteurs
les plus rayonnants de sa génération.
Et l'un des plus secrets.
Pour Studio, il a bien voulu se dévoiler.
Le Népal, Hollywood,
River Phoenix, l'innocence...

キアヌ・リーブス

Linda & Kyle
Photographs by Steven Meisel

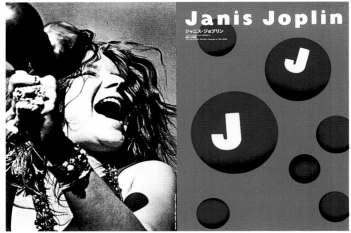

Janis Joplin
ジャニス・ジョプリン

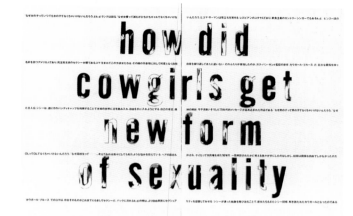

CUT

AS EXCLUSIVELY VISUAL magazines continue to grow throughout the world, the question is how to distinguish one from another, and how to distinguish one issue from the next. *Cut*, a multilingual interview magazine devoted to the movie and music businesses, has gone the route of minimal(ist) typography framing large, full-bleed pictures. Startling crops and jarring juxtapositions are key to making this magazine into a cinematic, print experience. And yet, how can the magazine maintain its own personality when it often uses well-known vintage pictures — like those of Jimi Hendrix or Janis Joplin? The answer is that each issue of *Cut* is on a special theme (such as violence, drugs, French films, etc.), and so the images are deliberately arranged to be consistent within the issue in which they appear. Actually, *Cut* is more like an exhibition between covers than a conventional magazine. Each feature flows into the next with the introduction typographic spread serving as a kind of intermission between galleries. In addition the typography is often designed in a photographic manner (such as placing images behind letters) to conform to the overall gestalt of the magazine. *Cut* is best defined by its strong pictorial presence and typographic restraint.

PUBLISHER
ROCKIN' ON, INC.
ART DIRECTOR
HIDEKI NAKAJIMA
DESIGNER
HIDEKI NAKAJIMA
TYPOGRAPHER
HIDEKI NAKAJIMA
PHOTOGRAPHERS
COLOMBIA
DALLEN KEITH
JEFFREY THURNHER
BRUCE WEBER

BY JAY MARTEL

On "The Larry Sanders Show," Garry Shandling turns the talk-show brouhaha into the funniest thing on TV

>>> Ideally, the first sentence of an article about Garry Shandling would set a provocative scene – such as Shandling calling his co-workers "fucking idiots" – before settling down to the more mundane details about the life of a self-referential comedian and sometime talk-show host, the same Garry Shandling who played a self-possessed comedian on the TV show It's Garry Shandling's Show and who now plays a self-absorbed TV talk-show host on the TV show The Larry Sanders Show, the same 44-year-old television auteur who has managed to turn selfness into a new TV form, the narcissitcom, without being self-indulgent and is now taking his act to the movies. But now it's too late. >>>

TRUE LIES

SLIPPIN' PITT AROUND ON THE ROAD WITH BRAD

PHOTOGRAPHS BY MARK SELIGER

TRENT REZNOR OF NINE INCH NAILS PREACHES THE DARK GOSPEL OF SEX, PAIN AND ROCK & ROLL
LOVE IT TO DEATH
BY JONATHAN GOLD

Tables sprout candles in the darkened control room as thick and as numerous as mushrooms on a dank forest floor, and miniskirted department-store mannequins are scattered about in various states of bon-

PHOTOGRAPH BY ANTON CORBIJN

PUBLISHER
WENNER MEDIA
ART DIRECTOR
FRED WOODWARD
DESIGNERS
GAIL ANDERSON
FRED WOODWARD
PHOTOGRAPHERS
ANTON CORBIJN
MARK SELIGER
ILLUSTRATORS
GARY KELLEY
ROBERT RISKO

MOVIES THE DYING GAME
BY PETER TRAVERS

INTERVIEW WITH THE VAMPIRE

STARRING
TOM CRUISE, BRAD PITT, ANTONIO BANDERAS, STEPHEN REA, KIRSTEN DUNST AND CHRISTIAN SLATER

WRITTEN BY
ANNE RICE

DIRECTED BY
NEIL JORDAN

WARNER BROS.

ILLUSTRATION BY GARY KELLEY

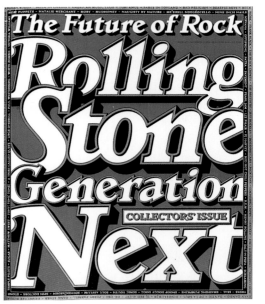

The Future of Rock
Rolling Stone
Generation
Next
COLLECTORS' ISSUE

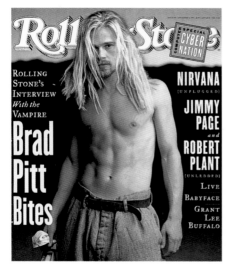

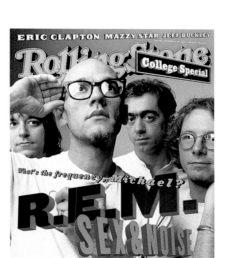

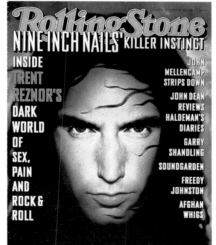

ROLLING STONE

WHEN *ROLLING STONE* approached its middle age eight years ago, it reprised many of the classic design characteristics which had been allowed to atrophy for one reason or another over time. Yet this was not nostalgia. *Rolling Stone*'s design direction does not retreat into the past but builds upon the foundations of imaginative typography and striking photography. What distinguishes *Rolling Stone* from other magazines is that its layouts are based on ideas — playful, historical, and unconventional — rather than knee-jerk responses to the latest computer font or trick. Two decades ago *Rolling Stone*'s key competitors were *Circus*, *Creem*, and *Rock* which more or less covered the same subjects from different perspectives. *Rolling Stone* was the principle outlet for news, reviews, and commentary while the others approached rock and roll as fashion. *Rolling Stone*'s format underscored the word, the others emphasized pictures. Today *Rolling Stone* is even more mature, but it would be erroneous to say that its format is only appropriate for a late-thirty- or forty-something audience. Nevertheless there are younger constituencies that respond to different editorial content and design. Not every rock and roll aficionado wants news and analysis when squibs and gossip will do. Not every music fan cares about design elegance, in fact some say it's an anachronism. And yet *Rolling Stone* is an institution that sets standards and styles. Therefore, any discussion of contemporary music magazine design must begin here.

PUBLISHER
WENNER MEDIA
ART DIRECTOR
FRED WOODWARD
DESIGNERS
LEE BEARSON
FRED WOODWARD
PHOTOGRAPHERS
MATT MAHURIN
MARK SELIGER
ILLUSTRATOR
PHILIP BURKE

SPY

IF ONE MAGAZINE can be credited with defining the style of magazine design for the mid-1980s, *Spy* is that magazine. Originally, this satiric journal of urban politics, culture and society, broke the mold of traditional magazine formatting by introducing a major front-of-the-book section comprised of various levels of factoids, short takes, and info-graphics. Often compared to a polyglot manuscript, the various type styles and families characterized different kinds of information presented on a single page or spread. This clash of typography was at once jarring and eye-catching, forcing the reader to navigate differently than with a conventional linear approach. *Spy* evolved under various art directors and designers, but it always maintained an irreverent editorial stance that was underscored by a smart, though decidedly tongue-in-cheek design. Feature articles included photographs or illustrations that underscored the satiric, and at times muckraking nature of the publication. Not always elegant, these layouts borrowed from and added a sophisticated twist to the sensationalistic layout of the tabloids. But if *Spy* will be noted for just one major contribution, it is the witty (and totally truthful) info-graphics in which silhouetted heads of celebrities are used as icons. These graphics, now a staple in newspapers and magazines, present fascinating data in visually accessible ways.

PUBLISHER
SPY MAGAZINE
ART DIRECTOR
ALEXANDER ISLEY
DESIGNERS
CATHERINE GILMORE-BARNES
ALEXANDER KNOWLTON
PHOTOGRAPHERS
CHRIS CALLIS
DEBORAH FEINGOLD
JOE McNALLY/WHEELER PICTURES
NEIL SELKIRK

TENSION

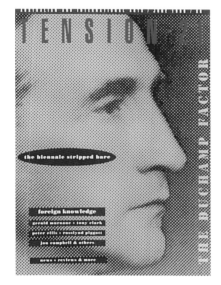

THE TITLE OF THIS arts and politics magazine suggests creative dissonance, cultural warfare, intellectual rigor, and a state of being that often produces great art. *Tension* also describes the magazine's design; a taught assemblage of type and image that is at once tightly controlled and constantly renewed. *Tension* began as a "homemade hobby," says its designer, "produced by a small group of people in the same flat." Because it was started as a "personal creative act, rather than a business venture, we had the freedom to evolve, make mistakes, and take risks." The equality between editor and designer contributed to a more "personal" graphic response than most similar publications. *Tension* is noteworthy for its continually changing covers — *Tension*/5 is a tightly packed type block, *Tension*/15 is a Philip Guston drawing sandwiched between type bars, and *Tension*/21 is a tightly cropped portrait — each with different logos. Interior layouts are individually solved puzzles that eschew any semblance of a standard grid. Produced on a shoestring budget, the art and photography is not commissioned, but are framed in such a skillful way that even the old chestnuts appear fresh.

PUBLISHER
XTENSION
ART DIRECTOR
TERENCE HOGAN
DESIGNER
TERENCE HOGAN
ARTISTS
PAUL BOSTON
BRETT COLQUHOUN
PHILIP GUSTON
DAVID SALLE
EDITORS
ROBIN BARDEN
ASHLEY CRAWFORD
RAY EDGAR
PHOTOGRAPHERS
WILLIAM CLAXTON
MARTIN KANTOR

A MONG HER

AFTER ALL THE CLOWNS
HAVE GONE TO BED

BUFFALO SOLDIERS

PUBLISHER
TIME INC. MAGAZINES
CREATIVE DIRECTOR
GARY KOEPKE
ART DIRECTOR
DIDDO RAMM
DESIGNER
DIDDO RAMM
PHOTOGRAPHERS
RUVEN AFANADOR
REISIG & TAYLOR
DAN WINTERS
CHRISTIAN WITKIN

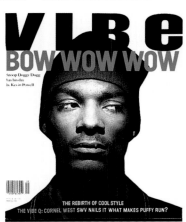

VIBe
BOW WOW WOW

Snoop Doggy Dogg
has his day
by Kevin Powell

THE REBIRTH OF COOL STYLE
THE VIBE Q: CORNEL WEST SWV NAILS IT WHAT MAKES PUFFY RUN?

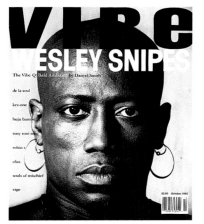

VIBe
WESLEY SNIPES

The Vibe Q: Bald Ambition by Danyel Smith

de la soul
krs-one
buju banton
tony toni tone
robin s
efua
souls of mischief
rage

$2.95 October 1993

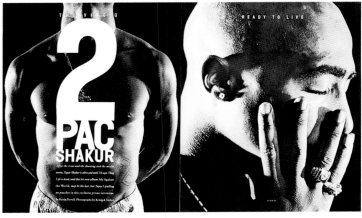

2 PAC SHAKUR

READY TO LIVE

After the trial and the shooting and the media
storm, Tupac Shakur is alive and well. Hi says, Thug
Life is dead, and that his new album, Me Against
the World, may be his last, but Tupac's pulling
no punches in this exclusive prison interview.
by Kevin Powell. Photographs by Reisig & Taylor

THE TROUBLE WITH WESLEY

Wesley Snipes crashes motorcycles, packs a semiautomatic,
and beats up the bad guys. Onscreen and off, Danyel Smith watches the first black action
hero on his day off from living the life of a Hollywood bad boy.

Photographs by Dan Winters

148

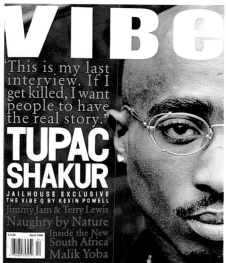

FEATURES
OCTOBER 1994 • VOLUME 2, NUMBER 8

PUBLISHER
TIME INC. MAGAZINES
ART DIRECTOR
DIDDO RAMM
DESIGNER
DIDDO RAMM
PHOTOGRAPHERS
BEN INGHAM
DANA LIXENBERG
REISIG & TAYLOR
EVERARD WILLIAMS JR.

USA

VIBE

DISTINGUISHING ITSELF from other music magazines, yet toeing the line between edge and mainstream, *Vibe* has successfully set a standard for the visual manifestation of hip hop or what it's editors call "urban culture." Although it conforms to the conventions of magazine makeup — clearly defined departments and a feature well — its typographic and photographic styles are distinctive. *Vibe* uses a limited typographic range — mostly bold gothics, like the logo, with the occasional serif face used for relief. The primary typography pounds like the hip hop beat, while the other faces serve as alternative melodies. The imagery is of the in-your-face school; subjects often stare directly into the lens, especially on the "wanted" posterlike covers, to make contact with the reader. Casual stances are kept to a minimum in favor of the monumental pose. Pacing in the editorial well is cinematic, often moving from quiet openers (with a generous amount of white space) to full-page bleeds, to text heavy spreads. Skewed type around photographs is a common conceit, and while it sometimes impedes easy reading, it serves to unify all the elements on a page into a single artwork. Although printed in full color, *Vibe* carefully avoids being slick in order to keep its street-smart aura.

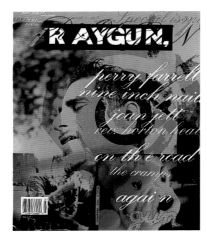

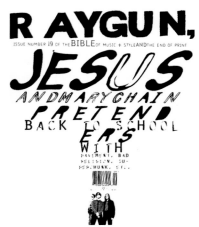

RAYGUN HAS succeeded in fundamentally reinventing the rock and roll magazine, if only visually, to appeal to a younger audience. It tests reader tolerance under stress; it is graphic performance art; it defines the '90s aesthetic through computer manipulations, printing contortions, and neo-expressionist visualizations, and is therefore a touchstone for those born into a wired world. *RayGun*'s graphic design is not transparent, and so it has forced its readers to confront issues of legibility, balance, harmony, and the key word of the '90s, fonts. Like the perceptual games played by the psychedelic artists of the '60s who broke all the rules in order to create cultural codes that only their constituents could decipher, its codes challenge the very basis of how people are taught to read books and magazines. Yet it also conforms to how people are forced to read the constant barrage of messages, advertisements, and graffiti on the streets and airwaves. It's anarchic look and computer in-jokes (for those who identify with the magazine), the non-hierarchical structure, graffitiesque layering, randomly skewed columns, and obliterated typefaces characterize the moment. *RayGun* defined a genre, mannerism, and style that is very difficult for others to break through.

PUBLISHER
**RAYGUN
PUBLISHING, INC.**
ART DIRECTOR
DAVID CARSON
DESIGNERS
**DAVID CARSON
SHAUN WOLFE**
PHOTOGRAPHERS
**A.J. BANTON
COLIN BELL
DAN CONWAY
H. FERGUSON
JASON LAMOTTE
MELODIE McDANIEL
AARON TUCKER
L. WIRTZ**
ILLUSTRATORS
**JENNIFER JESSE
SHAUN WOLFE**

PUBLISHER
**RAYGUN
PUBLISHING, INC.**

ART DIRECTOR
DAVID CARSON

DESIGNERS
**DAVID CARSON

SHAUN WOLFE**

PHOTOGRAPHERS
**COLIN BELL

GLEN ERLER

KEVIN KERSLAKE

CHARLES PURVIS

ALBERT WATSON**

ILLUSTRATORS
**DANIEL CONWAY

CHRISTIAN NORTHEAST

MARK TODD**

LETTERERS
**CALEF BROWN

MARCUS BURLILE**

PUBLISHER
L.O.C. ASSOCIATES, L.P.
ART DIRECTOR
DAVID HERBICK
DESIGNER
DAVID HERBICK
PHOTOGRAPHERS
BIBLIOTHÈQUE
NATIONALE DE FRANCE
EDWARD S. CURTIS
ILLUSTRATOR
C.F. PAYNE

USA

CIVILIZATION

A MAGAZINE THAT has to use historical images as the core of its visual content runs the risk of looking musty. Such was the challenge faced by the designers of *Civilization*, the journal of the Library of Congress, whose mission was to "explore historical and cultural connections to contemporary issues" by using this huge institution's vast documentary resources. The challenge extended to making a magazine that would avoid the stuffy appearance of academic journals as well as be flexible enough to accommodate all types of visual material. Avoiding fussiness, *Civilization*'s color palette and typography are limited. The result is a clean, rather classic look, "to be expected in a magazine associated with the Library of Congress," says its designer. But it is undeniably contemporary in the application of playful typographic and visual features. The magazine is indeed a treasure trove of the Library's holdings: a "Portfolio" of as many as 16 pages reveals the rich and varied print and photographic collections; "Curiosities" combines an image-dominant format with humor to showcase the unexpected holdings. Designed for a "highly educated and relatively affluent" audience, *Civilization* is conservative but nevertheless has a flair for the eccentric.

The POWER *of* CULTURE

The treasures of the Bibliothèque Nationale, on display at the Library of Congress, reveal that ◆ *the written word has been the fulcrum of French political life* ◆ BY ALICE KAPLAN

Info
As a media baron, Ben Franklin did well by doing good
Highwayman
By WALTER ISAACSON

PUBLISHER
L.O.C. ASSOCIATES, L.P.
ART DIRECTOR
DAVID HERBICK
DESIGNER
DAVID HERBICK
PHOTOGRAPHERS
EDWARD S. CURTIS
SEIJI FUKASAWA
WILLIAM GOTTLIEB
RUSSELL LEE
PAINTERS
KARL BODMER
JOHN WHITE
ILLUSTRATOR
JOHN H. HOWARD

Portfolio

Russell Lee's photos of a Louisiana
state fair capture the

spirit of the common man

BY NICHOLAS LEMANN

Watching the
parade in
Donaldsonville,
1938; and setting
up the Ferris
wheel

Cultures At War

A NEW BOOK AND AN
EIGHT-HOUR CBS
DOCUMENTARY VIEW
THE SETTLEMENT OF
THE NEW WORLD
THROUGH INDIAN EYES
BY JAMES CONAWAY

The death of Tecumseh, in an 1833 print, *inset,
from left:* Osage woman and child; No-Tin, a
Chippewa chief; Navajo girl, photo by Edward S.
Curtis; detail of Inuit woman and child, *watercolor
by John White;* Mallow Hare Bear, a Sioux leader,
by Edward S. Curtis; detail of a print of
Wahunsenaca, a Mosquakie, by Karl Bodmer

CIVILIZATION

JAN·FEB 1995
$4.50 / Can. $5.50

Confessions
of a
Burned-Out
Biographer
by
PHYLLIS
ROSE

Russell
Lee's
Louisiana
People
by
NICHOLAS
LEMANN

Whistler
v.
Ruskin
by
LINCOLN
CAPLAN

In Praise
of
Huck Finn
by
LANCE
MORROW

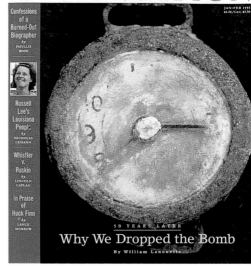

50 YEARS LATER

Why We Dropped the Bomb
By William Lanouette

PORTFOLIO
FROM THE COLLECTIONS OF THE LIBRARY OF CONGRESS

In nightclubs and concert halls, William Gottlieb captured
the most intimate moments of America's indigenous music

The Faces of Jazz

BY W. ROYAL STOKES

THELONIOUS
MONK AT
MINTON'S
PLAYHOUSE,
C. 1948

CIVILIZATION

JULY·AUG 1995
$4.50 / Can. $5.50

Inside the
Times
Book
Review
by
REBECCA
PEPPER
SINKLER

Defining
the Young
Nation
by
JOHN R.
STILGOE

The
Photos
That
Shocked
Victorians
by
RICHARD
A. KAYE

Thoreau's
Literary
Family
by
NOEL
PERRIN

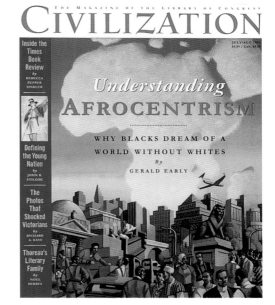

Understanding
AFROCENTRISM

WHY BLACKS DREAM OF A
WORLD WITHOUT WHITES
By
GERALD EARLY

DIRECTORY

21•C
The Australian
Commission for the
Future Ltd.
P.O. Box 115
Carlton South, Victoria
Australia 3053

A. Arefin
611 Broadway, Suite 840
New York, NY 10012
USA

AIRIC
(Architectural Research &
Criticism)
Atlas of the City
Publications
20 Shallmar Boulevard,
Suite 304
Toronto, Ontario M5N 1J5
Canada

Abitare
Editrice Abitare Segesta
corso Monforte, 15
20122 Milano
Italy

Adams + Associates
Design Consultants Inc.
25 A Morrow Avenue,
Suite 303
Toronto, Ontario M6R 2H9
Canada

AdD:
Casa de Ideias
Av. Candido de Abreu,
526-16-Torre B-102-603
Curitiba, PR
Brazil 80.530-905

Alexander Isley Design
4 Old Mill Road
Redding, CT 06896
USA

ANY
(Architecture New York)
Anyone Corporation
40 West 25th Street
New York, NY 10010
USA

Archis
Netherlands Architecture
Institute/Misset
Publishers
Jongkindstraat 5
3015 CG Rotterdam
The Netherlands

Art Issues.
The Foundation
for Advanced Critical
Studies, Inc.
8721 Santa Monica
Boulevard, #6
Los Angeles, CA 90069
USA

Atlanta Art & Design, Inc.
511 King Street West,
Suite 400
Toronto, Ontario M5V 1K4
Canada

Azure
Azure Publishing Inc.
2 Silver Avenue
Toronto, Ontario M6R 3A2
Canada

Big
Location Printing Big.S.L.
61 East 8th Street,
Suite 167
New York, NY 10003
USA

Blind Spot
Kim Zorn Caputo/
Lexington Labs
49 West 23rd Street
New York, NY 10010
USA

Blueprint
Wordsearch
Publishing Inc.
26 Cramer Street
London W1M 3He
England

C Magazine
C Arts Publishing &
Production, Inc.
988 Queen Street West
Toronto, Ontario M6J 1H1
Canada

Canadian Art
The Canadian Art
Foundation
70 The Esplanade,
2nd Floor
Toronto, Ontario M5E 1M1
Canada

Civilization Magazine
666 Pennsylvania Avenue
SE, #303
Washington, DC 20003
USA

Colors
Colors Magazine SRL
Via di Panico 72
00186 Rome
Italy

Concrete Design
Communications Inc.
2 Silver Avenue
Toronto, Ontario M6R 3A2
Canada

Cut
Rockin' On, Inc.
N-6F, N.E.S. Building,
22-14
Sakuragaoka-cho
Shibuya-Ku, Tokyo 150
Japan

Dance Ink
Dance Ink, Inc.
145 Central Park West
New York, NY 10023
USA

David Carson Design
432 F Street, #503
San Diego, CA 92101
USA

Design Writing Research
J. Abbott Miller
214 Sullivan Street, #4C
New York, NY 10012
USA

Dialogue
Norbord Industries
1 Toronto Street
Toronto, Ontario M5C 2W4
Canada

Discover
Walt Disney Magazine
Publishing Group Inc.
114 Fifth Avenue
New York, NY 10011
USA

El Mundo Magazine
Unidad Editorial S.A.
Pradillo 42
28002 Madrid
Spain

Emigre
4475 "D" Street
Sacramento, CA 95819
USA

Entertainment Weekly
Time Inc.
1675 Broadway
New York, NY 10019
USA

Esquire
Hearst Corporation
250 West 55th Street,
8th Floor
New York, NY 10019
USA

Eye
Emap Business
Communications
33-39 Bowling Green Lane
London, EC1R ODA
England

Frost Design
2A Shelford Place
London, N166 9HX
England

FYI
Forbes Inc.
660 Fifth Avenue
New York, NY 10011
USA

Garbage
Dovetale Publishers
2 Main Street
Gloucester, MA 01930
USA

Garden Design
Meigher Communications
100 Avenue of the
Americas, 7th Floor
New York, NY 10013
USA

Global
Bull H.N. Information
Systems, Inc.
Bull Technology Park
Billerica, MA 01821
USA

Gráfica
Casa de Ideias
Av. Candido de Abreu
526-16-Torre B-1602-603
Curitiba, PR
Brazil 80.530-905

Graphis
Graphis US, Inc.
141 Lexington Avenue
New York, NY 10016
USA

Guggenheim Magazine
Solomon R. Guggenheim
Museum
1071 Fifth Avenue
New York, NY 10128
USA

Harper's Bazaar
The Hearst Corporation
250 West 55th Street
New York, NY 10019
USA

Health
The Health Publishing
Group
301 Howard Street,
18th Floor
San Francisco, CA 94105
USA

Herman DeVries
Van Eeghenstraat 185
1071 GD Amsterdam
The Netherlands

Interior Design Outlook
Association of
Registered Interior
Designers of Ontario
717 Church Street
Toronto, Ontario
M4W 2M5
Canada

Johnston & Wolverton
1314 NW Irving #702
Portland, OR 97209
USA

Koepke International
Box 5360
10 Oakes Avenue, #3
Magnolia, MA 01930
USA

L'Amateur de Bordeaux S.E.S.
(Société d'Éditions Spécialisées)
22, rue des Reculettes
75013 Paris
France

L'Amateur de Cigare S.E.S.
(Société d'Éditions Spécialisées)
22, rue des Reculettes
75013 Paris
France

Library of Congress, L.P.
475 Park Avenue
New York, NY 10016
USA

Life
Time Inc. Magazines
1271 Avenue of the Americas
New York, NY 10020
USA

Lotus Quaterly
Lotus Development Corporation
55 Cambridge Parkway
Cambridge, MA 02142
USA

Manhattan File
News Communications, Inc.
594 Broadway, Suite 500
New York, NY 10012
USA

Mâp
Map Publications Inc.
459 West Broadway, Suite 2NW
New York, NY 10012
USA

Martha Stewart Living
Time Inc.
20 West 43rd Street
New York, NY 10036
USA

McCallum/Martel
988 Queen Street West
Toronto, Ontario M6J 1H1
Canada

Metalsmith
Society of North American Goldsmiths
5009 Londonderry Drive
Tampa, FL 33647
USA

Metropolis
Bellerophon Publications Inc.
177 East 87th Street, #504
New York, NY 10128
USA

Miran Design Inc.
Rua Jesuino Lopes, 390
Curitiba, PR
Brazil 80.310-620

Mojo
Emap Metro Ltd.
Mappin House
4 Winsley Street
London, W1N 7AR
England

Mondo 2000
Fun City Megamedia
P.O. Box 10171
Berkeley, CA 94709
USA

Nickelodeon
1515 Broadway
New York, NY 10036
USA

Norlen & Associates
1715 N. Fair Oaks, #6
South Pasadena, CA 91030
USA

Nozone
Knickerbocker
P.O. Box 1124
Knickerbocker Station
New York, NY 10002
USA

O-Zone
Casa de Ideias
Av. Candido de Abreu, 526-16-Torre B-102-603
Curitiba, PR
Brazil 80.530-905

Paul Davis Studio
14 East 4th Street, #504
New York, NY 10012
USA

Pentagram Design
212 Fifth Avenue
New York, NY 10010
USA

Pictopia
Fantagraphics Books, Inc.
7563 Lake City Way
Seattle, WA 98115
USA

Plunkett + Kuhr
P.O. Box 2237
Park City, Utah 84060
USA

PM Design
Patrick Mitchell
8 Blackburn Center
Gloucester, MA 01930
USA

Pushpin Group, Inc.
215 Park Avenue South, Suite 1300
New York, NY 10003
USA

R Company
Rhonda Rubenstein
143 Avenue B, Suite 12G
New York, NY 10009
USA

Rampazzo et Associés
9, rue Fénelou
75010 Paris
France

Raygun
Raygun Publishing, Inc.
2110 Main Street 100
Santa Monica, CA 90405
USA

Regional Review
Federal Reserve Bank of Boston
P.O. Box 2076
Boston, MA 02106
USA

Rolling Stone
Wenner Media
1290 Avenue of the Americas, 2nd Floor
New York, NY 10104
USA

Ronn Campisi Design
118 Newbury Street
Boston, MA 02116
USA

Rubber Blanket
Rubber Blanket Press
P.O. Box 3067
Uptown Station
Hoboken, NJ 07030
USA

Saveur
Meigher Communications
100 Avenue of the Americas, 7th Floor
New York, NY 10013
USA

Say
Say Magazine
1314 NW Irving #702
Portland, OR 97209
USA

Shiffman/Young Design Group
7421 Beverly Boulevard, #4
Los Angeles, CA 90036
USA

Spy
Sussex Publishing Co., Inc.
49 E. 21st Street
New York, NY 10010
USA

Studio Lupi
Via Vigevano, 39
20100 Milano
Italy

Terence Hogan Design
2/42 Cromwell Road
South Yarra, Melbourne
Australia 3141

The Boston Globe Magazine
The Boston Globe
135 Morrissey Boulevard
Boston, MA 02107
USA

The New York Times Magazine
The New York Times Co.
229 West 43rd Street
New York, NY 10036
USA

The Washington Post Magazine
1150 15th Street NW
Washington, DC 20005
USA

U&lc
International Typeface Corporation
866 Second Avenue, 3rd Floor
New York, NY 10017
USA

Via Marketing & Design
34 Danforth Street, Suite 309
Portland, ME 04101
USA

Vibe
Vibe Magazine
205 Lexington Avenue, 3rd Floor
New York, NY 10016
USA

Vignelli Associates
475 Tenth Avenue
New York, NY 10018
USA

Visionaire
Visionaire Publishing Co.
58 Watts Street, Rear Bldg.
New York, NY 10013
USA

W
Fairchild Publications
7 West 34th Street
New York, NY 10001
USA

Weisz Yang Dunkelberger, Inc.
661 Wilton Road
Westport, CT 06880
USA

Wired
Wired Ventures Limited
520 Third Street
San Francisco, CA 94107
USA

World Art
G + B Arts International, 1st Floor
478 Chapel Street
South Yarra
Australia

World Tour
Dun & Bradstreet Software
550 Cochituate Road
Framingham, MA 01701
USA

INDEX

PHOTOGRAPHERS

158

ILLUSTRATORS/ARTISTS

The authors would like to thank Deby Harding, our editor, for
her dedicated work on this difficult project. Thanks also to
Mark Serchuck, our publisher; Penny Sibal, managing director;
Susan Kapsis, managing editor; Richard Liu, technical director;
and Frank Zanone, editorial assistant. We are indebted to
Daniel Drennan for his electronic production expertise; to Geoff
Spear for his signature photography; to Christine Thompson
for her research; to Tom Mylroie for his publication photos; and
to all the designers, art directors, and editors whose work is
represented, without whose cooperation this book would have
been impossible.